A POETICAL COOK-BOOK BY M. J. M.

Almost everybody knows the lines "we may live without friends; we may live without books; but civilized man cannot live without *cooks*..." Some people even know that these lines are by Owen Meredith, and a few people know that the poem from which they are taken has the title *Lucile,* but very few people know that the quotation became very famous a hundred some years ago because it was facing the title page of M. J. M.'s *Poetical Cook-Book* which was printed in 1864.

Hiding behind the M. J. M. was Maria J. Moss, who dedicated her book to the Sanitary Fair in Philadelphia.

A very interesting book indeed, full of poetry—some good, some charming, some childish, some bad, but all collected and assembled with charm and gusto. As a cookery book, it was a very popular and very useful book in its time. Some of its recipes are today still as good as they were when written, others would be any modern homemaker's nightmare...

> Hang a fifty pound turtle in your kitchen and while you are cutting the flesh out from it, gently simmer a little consomme from a mere twenty pounds of veal...

On the other hand, her perch with wine is still a gourmet's delight. The capon couldn't be prepared better by anyone, and her macaroni gratin and her omelette souffle are just as perfect today as when the recipes were written and cooked all over in the war-ridden country.

Our kitchen range or stove was not yet invented, and all the cooking was done in front of or over charcoal. Of course, this is no problem today; the broiler (if not a charcoal broiler) is standard equipment in every kitchen.

For some of the ingredients, today's homemaker would shop in vain, but many substitutes are available. Even if you never try to cook anything from the book, you can just browse through it to enjoy the fragrance and flavor of by-gone days.

LOUIS SZATHMARY
April 25, 1972

We may live without poetry, music, and art;
We may live without conscience and live without heart;
We may live without friends; we may live without books;
But civilized man cannot live without *cooks*.
He may live without books—what is knowledge but grieving?
He may live without hope—what is hope but deceiving?
He may live without love—what is passion but pining?
But where is the man who can live without *dining*?

OWEN MEREDITH'S "LUCILE."

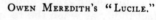

A

POETICAL COOK-BOOK.

BY

[MARIA J. MOSS]

" I REQUEST you will prepare
To your own taste the bill of fare;
At present, if to judge I'm able,
The finest works are of the table.
I should prefer the cook just now
To Rubens or to Gerard Dow."

PHILADELPHIA:

CAXTON PRESS OF C. SHERMAN, SON & CO.
1864.

ARNO PRESS / A NEW YORK TIMES COMPANY

This volume was selected for republication
by Louis Szathmary

Introduction Copyright © 1972
by Louis Szathmary

Reprinted from a copy in
The Cornell University Library

Library of Congress Catalog Card Number: 72-3979
International Standard Book Numbers:
Clothbound 0-405-02213-1
Paperbound 0-405-02214-X

Reprint Edition 1972

Manufactured in the United States of America

DEDICATION.

" What's under this cover ?
   For cookery's a secret."—Moore.

When I wrote the following pages, some years back
at Oak Lodge, as a pastime, I did not think it would be
of service to my fellow-creatures, for our suffering sol-
diers, the sick, wounded, and needy, who have so nobly
fought our country's cause, to maintain the flag of our
great Republic, and to prove among Nations that a Free
Republic is not a myth.   With these few words I dedi-
cate this book to the Sanitary Fair to be held in
Philadelphia, June, 1864.

March, 1864.

1*

THROUGH tomes of fable and of dream
I sought an eligible theme;
But none I found, or found them shared
Already by some happier bard,
Till settling on the current year
I found the far-sought treasure near.
A theme for poetry, you see—
A theme t' ennoble even me,
In memorable forty-three.

Oh, Dick! you may talk of your writing and reading,
Your logic and Greek, but there is nothing like feeding.
MOORE.

Upon ſinging and cookery, Bobby, of course,
Standing up for the latter Fine Art in full force.
MOORE.

Are these the *choice dishes* the Doctor has sent us?
Heaven sends us good meats, but the Devil sends cooks.

That my life, like the German, may be
"Du lit a la table, de la table au lit."—MOORE.

TO THE READER.

Though cooks are often men of pregnant wit,
Through niceness of their subject few have writ.
'Tis a sage question, if the art of cooks
Is lodg'd by nature or attain'd by books?
That man will never frame a noble treat,
Whose whole dependence lies in some *receipt*.
Then by pure nature everything is spoil'd,—
She knows no more than stew'd, bak'd, roast, and boil'd.
When art and nature join, the effect will be,
Some nice *ragout*, or *charming fricasee*.
What earth and waters breed, or air inspires,
Man for his palate fits by torturing fires.
But, though my edge be not too nicely set,
Yet I another's appetite may whet;
May teach him when to buy, when season's pass'd,
What's stale, what choice, what plentiful, what waste,

And lead him through the various maze of taste.
The fundamental principle of all
Is what ingenious cooks the *relish* call;
For when the market sends in loads of food,
They all are tasteless till *that* makes them good.
Besides, 'tis no ignoble piece of care,
To know for whom it is you would prepare.
You'd please a friend, or reconcile a brother,
A testy father, or a haughty mother;
Would mollify a judge, would cram a squire,
Or else some smiles from court you would desire;
Or would, perhaps, some hasty supper give,
To show the splendid state in which you live.
Pursuant to that interest you propose,
Must all your wines and all your meat be chose.
Tables should be like pictures to the sight,
Some dishes cast in shade, some spread in light;
Some at a distance brighten, some near hand,
Where ease may all their delicace command;
Some should be moved when broken, others last
Through the whole treat, incentive to the taste.
Locket, by many labors feeble grown,
Up from the kitchen call'd his eldest son;
Though wise thyself (says he), though taught by me,
Yet fix this sentence in thy memory:

There are some certain things that don't excel,
And yet we say are tolerably well.
There's many worthy men a lawyer prize,
Whom they distinguish as of middle size,
For pleading well at bar or turning books;
But this is not, my son, the fate of cooks,
From whose mysterious art true pleasure springs,
To stall of garters, and to throne of kings.
A simple scene, a disobliging song,
Which no way to the main design belong,
Or were they absent never would be miss'd,
Have made a well-wrought comedy be hiss'd;
So in a feast, no intermediate fault
Will be allow'd; but if not best, 'tis nought.
If you, perhaps, would try some dish unknown,
Which more peculiarly you'd make your own,
Like ancient sailors, still regard the coast,—
By venturing out too far you may be lost.
By roasting that which your forefathers boil'd,
And broiling what they roasted, much is spoil'd.
That cook to American palates is complete,
Whose savory hand gives turn to common meat.
Far from your parlor have your kitchen placed,
Dainties may in their working be disgraced.
In private draw your poultry, clean your tripe,
And from your eels their slimy substance wipe.

Let cruel offices be done by night,
For they who like the thing abhor the sight.
'Tis by his cleanliness a cook must please;
A kitchen will admit of no disease.
Were Horace, that great master, now alive,
A feast with wit and judgment he'd contrive,
As thus: Supposing that you would rehearse
A labor'd work, and every dish a verse,
He'd say, "Mend this and t'other line and this."
If after trial it were still amiss,
He'd bid you give it a new turn of face,
Or set some dish more curious in its place.
If you persist, he would not strive to move
A passion so delightful as self-love.
Cooks garnish out some tables, some they fill,
Or in a prudent mixture show their skill.
Clog not your constant meals; for dishes few
Increase the appetite when choice and new.
E'en they who will extravagance profess,
Have still an inward hatred for excess.
Meat forced too much, untouch'd at table lies;
Few care for carving trifles in disguise,
Or that fantastic dish some call *surprise*.
When pleasures to the eye and palate meet,
That cook has render'd his great work complete;

His glory far, like *sirloin knighthood*[1] flies
Immortal made, as *Kit-cat* by his pies.
Next, let discretion moderate your cost,
And when you treat, three courses be the most.
Let never fresh machines your pastry try,
Unless grandees or magistrates are by,
Then you may put *a dwarf into a pie.*[2]
Crowd not your table; let your number be
Not more than seven, and never less than three.
'Tis the *dessert* that graces all the feast,
For an ill end disparages the rest.
A thousand things well done, and one forgot,
Defaces obligation by that blot.
Make your transparent sweetmeats truly nice
With Indian sugar and Arabian spice.
And let your various creams encircled be
With swelling fruit just ravish'd from the tree.
The feast now done, discourses are renewed,
And witty arguments with mirth pursued;

[1] Charles I, dining one day off of a loin of beef, was so much pleased with it, knighted it.

[2] In the reign of Charles I, Jeffry Hudson (then seven or eight years old, and but eighteen inches in height) was served up to table in a cold pie at the Duke of Buckingham's, and as soon as he made his appearance was presented to the Queen.

The cheerful master, 'midst his jovial friends,
His glass to their best wishes recommends.
The grace cup follows: To the President's health
And to the country; Plenty, Peace, and Wealth!
Performing, then, the piety of grace,
Each man that pleases reassumes his place;
While at his gate, from such abundant store,
He showers his godlike blessings on the poor.

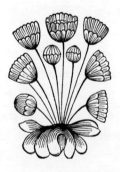

MISCELLANEOUS OBSERVATIONS

FOR THE USE OF THE

MISTRESS OF A FAMILY.

THE mistress of a family should always remember that the welfare and good management of the house depend on the eye of the superior, and, consequently, that nothing is too trifling for her notice, whereby waste may be avoided.

Many families have owed their prosperity full as much to the conduct and propriety of female arrangement, as to the knowledge and activity of the father.

All things likely to be wanted should be in readiness,— sugars of different qualities should be broken; currants washed, picked and dry in a jar; spice pounded, &c. Every article should be kept in that place best suited to it, as much waste may thereby be avoided. Vegetables

2

will keep best on a stone floor if the air be excluded. Dried meats, hams, &c., the same. All sorts of seeds for puddings, rice, &c., should be close-covered, to preserve from insects. Flour should be kept in a cool, perfectly dry room, and the bag being tied should be changed upside down and back every week, and well shaken. Carrots, parsnips, and beet-roots should be kept in sand for winter use, and neither they nor potatoes be cleared from the earth. Store onions preserve best hung up in a dry room. Straw to lay apples on should be quite dry, to prevent a musty taste. Tarragon gives the flavor of French cookery, and in high gravies should be added only a short time before serving.

Basil, savory, and knotted marjoram, or London thyme, to be used when herbs are ordered; but with discretion, as they are very pungent.

Celery seeds give the flavor of the plant to soups. Parsley should be cut close to the stalks, and dried on tins in a very cool oven; it preserves its flavor and color, and is very useful in winter. Artichoke bottoms, which have been slowly dried, should be kept in paper bags, and truffles, lemon-peel, &c., in a very dry place, ticketed.

Pickles and sweetmeats should be preserved from air : where the former are much used, small jars of each should be taken from the stock-jar, to prevent frequent opening.

Some of the lemons and oranges used for juice should

be pared first, to preserve the peel dry; some should be halved, and, when squeezed, the pulp cut out, and the outsides dried for grating.

If for boiling any liquid, the first way is best. When whites of eggs are used for jelly, or other purposes, contrive to have pudding, custards, &c., to employ the yolks also.

Gravies or soups put by, should be daily changed into fresh scalded pans.

If chocolate, coffee, jelly, gruel, bark, &c., be suffered to boil over, the strength is lost.

The cook should be charged to take care of jelly bags, tapes for the collared things, &c., which, if not perfectly scalded and kept dry, give an unpleasant flavor when next used.

Hard water spoils the color of vegetables; a pinch of pearlash or salt of wormwood will prevent that effect.

When sirloins of beef, loins of veal or mutton come in, part of the suet may be cut off for puddings, or to clarify; dripping will baste everything as well as butter, fowls and game excepted; and for kitchen pies nothing else should be used.

Meat and vegetables that the frost has touched should be soaked in cold water two or three hours before they are used, or more if much iced; when put into hot water, or to the fire until thawed, no heat will dress them properly.

Meat should be well examined when it comes in, in warm weather. In the height of the summer it is a very safe way to let meat that is to be salted lie an hour in cold water; then wipe it perfectly dry, and have ready salt, and rub it thoroughly into every part, leaving a handful over it besides. Turn it every day and rub the pickle in, which will make it ready for the table in three or four days; if it is desired to be very much corned, wrap it in a well-floured cloth, having rubbed it previously with salt. The latter method will corn fresh beef fit for table the day it comes in; but it must be put into the pot when the water boils.

If the weather permits, meat eats much better for hanging two or three days before it be salted.

The water in which meat has been boiled makes an excellent soup for the poor, when vegetables, oatmeal, or peas are added, and should not be cleared from the fat. Roast beef bones, or shank bones of ham, make fine peas soup, and should be boiled with the peas the day before eaten, that the fat may be removed. The mistress of the house will find many great advantages in visiting her larder daily before she orders the bill of fare; she will see what things require dressing, and thereby guard against their being spoiled. Many articles may be re dressed in a different form from that in which they are first served, and improve the appearance of the table without increasing the expense.

In every sort of provisions, the best of the kind goes farthest; cutting out most advantageously, and affording most nourishment.

Round of beef, fillet of veal, and leg of mutton, bear a higher price; but having more solid meat, deserve the preference. It is worth notice, however, that those joints which are inferior may be dressed as palatably, and being cheaper ought to be bought in turn; and when weighed with the prime pieces, the price of the latter is reduced.

In loins of meat, the long pipe which runs by the bone should be taken out, being apt to taint, as likewise the kernels of beef.

Rumps and aitch bones of beef are often bruised by the blows the drovers give, and that part always taints: avoid purchasing such.

The shank bones of mutton should be saved, and after soaking and bruising may be added to give richness to gravies and soups, and they are particularly nourishing for the sick.

Calves' tongues, salted, make a more useful dish than when dressed with the brains, which may be served without.

Some people like neats' tongues cured with the root, in which case they look much larger; but should the contrary be approved, the root must be cut off close to the gullet, next to the tongue, but without taking away the fat under the tongue. The root must be soaked in salt and water, and extremely well cleaned before it be dressed; and the tongue laid in salt for a night and day before pickled.

Great attention is requisite in salting meat, and in the country, where great quantities are cured, it is of still more importance. Beef and pork should be well sprinkled, and a few hours after hung to drain, before it be rubbed with the preserving salts; which mode, by cleansing the meat from the blood, tends to keep it from tasting strong; it should be turned daily, and, if wanted soon, rubbed. A salting tub may be used, and a cover should fit close. Those who use a good deal of salt will find it well to boil up the pickle, skim, and when cold pour it over meat that has been sprinkled and drained. In some families great loss is sustained by the spoiling of meat. If meat is brought from a distance in warm weather, the butcher should be charged to cover it close, and bring it early in the morning.

Mutton will keep long, by washing with vinegar the broad end of the leg; if any damp appears, wipe it immediately. If rubbed with salt lightly, it will not eat the worse.   Game is brought in when not likely to keep a day, in the cook's apprehension, yet may be preserved two or three days if wanted, by the following method:

If birds (woodcocks and snipes excepted, which must not be drawn), draw them, pick and take out the crop, wash them in two or three waters, and rub them with a little salt.   Have ready a large saucepan of boiling water, put the birds in it, and let them remain five minutes, moving it, that it may go through them. When all are finished, hang them by the heads in a cold place; when drained, pepper the inside and necks; when to be roasted, wash, to take off the pepper.   The most delicate birds, even grouse, may be kept this way, if not putrid.

Birds that live by suction, &c., bear being high: it is probable that the heat might cause them to taint more, as a free passage for the scalding water could not be obtained.

Fresh-water fish has often a muddy taste, to take off which, soak it in strong salt and water; or, if of a size to bear it, give it a scald in the same, after extremely good cleaning and washing.

In the following, and indeed all other receipts, though the quantities may be as accurately set down as possible, yet much must be left to the discretion of the persons who use them.

The different taste of people requires more or less of the flavor of spices, garlic, butter, &c., which can never be directed by general rules, and if the cook has not a good taste, and attention to that of her employers, not all the ingredients with which nature or art can furnish her will give an exquisite relish to her dishes.

The proper articles should be at hand, and she must proportion them until the true zest be obtained.

March, 1864.

Poetical Cook-Book.

SOUPS.

TURTLE SOUP.

Sons of Apicius! say, can Europe's seas,
Can aught the edible creation yield
Compare with *turtle*, boast of land and wave?
GRAINGER.

And, zounds! who would grudge
Turtle soup, though it came to five guineas the bowl?
MOORE.

THE day before you dress a turtle, chop the
herbs, and make the forcemeat; then, on the pre-
ceding evening, suspend the turtle by the two
hind fins with a cord, and put one round the neck
with a heavy weight attached to it to draw out
the neck, that the head may be cut off with more
ease; let the turtle hang all night, in which time
the blood will be well drained from the body.
Then, early in the morning, having your stoves
and plenty of hot water in readiness, take the
turtle, lay it on the table on its back, and with a

strong pointed knife cut round the under shell
(which is the callipee),—there are joints at each
end, which must be carefully found,—gently sepa-
rating it from the callipash (which is the upper
shell); be careful that in cutting out the gut you
do not break the gall. When the callipee and the
callipash are perfectly separated, take out that
part of the gut that leads from the throat; that
with the hearts put into a basin of water by themselves, the other interior part put away. Take
the callipee, and cut off the meat which adheres
to it in four quarters, laying it on a clean dish.
Take twenty pounds of veal, chop it up, and set it
in a large pot, as directed for espagnoles, putting
in the flesh of the turtle at the same time, with all
kinds of turtle herbs, carrots, onions, one pound
and a half of lean ham, peppercorns, salt, and a
little spice, and two bay leaves, leaving it to stew
till it take the color of espagnole; put the fins—the
skin scalded off—and hearts in, half an hour before
you fill it, with half water, and half beef stock, then
carefully skim it; put in a bunch of parsley, and
let it boil gently like consommé. While the turtle
is stewing, carefully scald the head, the callipee,
and all that is soft of the callipash, attentively
observing to take off the smallest skin that may
remain; put them with the gut into a large pot of
water to boil till tender; when so, take them out

and cut them in squares, putting them in a basin
by themselves till wanted for the soup. The next
thing is the thickening of the soup, which must be
prepared in the same manner as sauce tournée.
The turtle being well done, take out the fins and
hearts, and lay them on a dish; the whole of the
liquor must pass through a sieve into a large pan;
then with a ladle take off all the fat, put it into a
basin, then mix in the turtle liquor (a small quantity at a time), with the thickening made the same
as tournée; but it does not require to, neither
must it, be one-twentieth part as thick. Set it
over a brisk fire, and continue stirring till it boils.
When it has boiled gently for one hour put in the
callipee and callipash with the guts, hearts, and
some of the best of the meat and head, all cut in
squares, with the forcemeat balls and herbs, which
you should have ready chopped and stewed in
espagnole; the herbs and parsley, lemon, thyme,
marjoram, basil, savory, and a few chopped mushrooms.

It must be carefully attended to and skimmed,
and one hour and a half before dinner put in a
bottle of Madeira wine, and nearly half a bottle
of brandy, keeping it continually boiling gently,
and skimming it, then take a basin, put a little
cayenne into it, with the juice of six lemons
squeezed through a sieve. When the dinner is

wanted, skim the turtle, stir it well up, and put a little salt, if necessary; then stir the cayenne and lemon juice in, and ladle it into the tureen. This receipt will answer for a turtle between fifty and sixty pounds.

CHICKEN BROTH.

The *chicken broth* was brought at nine;
He then arose to ham and wine,
And, with a philosophic air,
Decided on the bill of fare.

Take the remaining parts of a chicken from which panada has been made, all but the rump; skin, and put them into the water it was first boiled in, with the addition of a little mace, onion, and a few pepper-corns, and simmer it. When of a good flavor, put to it a quarter of an ounce of sweet almond beaten with a spoonful of water; boil it a little while, and when cold take off the fat.

FISH.

TO STEW FISH WHITE.

His soup scientific,—his *fishes* quite prime;
His patés superb, and his cutlets sublime.
MOORE.

LET your fish be cleaned and salted; save your melts or kows. Cut three onions and parsley root, boil them in a pint of water; cut your fish in pieces to suit; take some clever sized pieces, cut them from the bone, chop them fine, mix with them the melts, crumbs of bread, a little ginger, one egg well beaten, leeks, green parsley, all made fine; take some bread, and make them in small balls; lay your fish in your stewpan, layer of fish and layer of onions; sprinkle with ginger, pour cold water over to cover your fish; let it boil till done, then lay your fish nicely on a dish. To make the sauce, take the juice of a large lemon and yolk of an egg, well beaten together, teaspoonful of flour; mix it gradually with half a pint of the water the fish was done in, then with all your water put in your balls; let it boil very quick; when done throw the balls and gravy over your fish.

3

ANOTHER WAY TO STEW FISH.

Behold, the dishes due appear!
Fish in the van, beef in the rear.
Ah! all the luxury of fish,
With scalding sauce.

Boil six onions in water till tender, strain, and cut them in slices. Put your fish, cut in slices, in a stewpan with a quart of water, salt, pepper, ginger and mace to suit taste; let it boil fifteen minutes; add the onions, and forcemeat balls made of chopped fish, grated bread, chopped onion, parsley, marjoram, mace, pepper, ginger and salt, and five eggs beat up with a spoon into balls, and drop them into the pan of fish when boiling; cover close for ten minutes, take it off the fire, and then add six eggs with the juice of five lemons; stir the gravy very slowly, add chopped parsley, and let it all simmer on a slow fire, keeping the pan in motion until it just boils, when it must be taken off quickly, or the sauce will break. A little butter or sweet oil added to the balls is an improvement. If you meet with good success in the cooking of this receipt, you will often have stewed fish.

PERCH WITH WINE.

Here haddock, hake, and flounders are,
And eels, and *perch*, and cod.

GREEN.

Having scalded and taken out the gills, put the perch into a stew-pan, with equal quantities of stock and white wine, a bay leaf, a clove of garlic, a bunch of parsley, and scallions, two cloves, and some salt.

When done, take out the fish, strain off the liquor, the dregs of which mix with some butter and a little flour; beat these up, set them on the fire, stewing till quite done, adding pepper, grated nutmeg, and a ball of anchovy butter. Drain the perch well, and dish them with the above sauce.

TO STEW FISH BROWN.

Here stay thy haste,
And with the *savory fish* indulge thy taste.

GAY.

Have your fish cleaned, the melts or kows being taken out whole; salt your fish, and let it lay half an hour. Cut your onions in slices, fry them with parsley-root, cut in long thin slices, in half a tea-

cup of sweet oil, till they become a fine brown.
Wash and dry your fish, cut it in pieces, put it in
your stewpan, layer of fish and layer of browned
onion, &c.   Take a quart of beer, half a pint of
vinegar, quarter pound of sugar, two tablespoonfuls powdered ginger, mixed well together, pour
over your fish till covered.   When putting your
fish in the pan, split the head in two, and place it
at the bottom, the smaller pieces on the top, the
rows uppermost; let them cook very quick.   Take
out your fish, lay it nicely on a dish, mix a little
flour in your gravy, give it a boil, throw it over
the fish, and let it stand to cool.

ROASTED STURGEON.

Your betters will despise you, if they see
Things that are far surpassing your degree;
Therefore beyond your substance never treat;
'Tis plenty, in small fortune, to be neat;
A widow has cold pie, nurse gives you cake,
From generous merchants ham or *sturgeon* take.
                                        KING.

Take a large piece of sturgeon, or a whole small
one, clean and skin it properly, lard it with eel
and anchovies, and marinade it in a white wine
marmalade.   Fasten it to the spit and roast it,

basting frequently with the marinade strained.
Let the fish be a nice color, and serve with a
pepper sauce.

BOILED SALMON.

Red speckled trouts, the *salmon's* silver jole,
The jointed lobster and unscaly sole,
And luscious scallops to allure the tastes
Of rigid zealots to delicious feasts;
Wednesdays and Fridays, you'll observe from hence,
Days when our sins were doomed to abstinence.

GAY.

Put on a fish-kettle, with spring water enough
to well cover the salmon you are going to dress, or
the salmon will neither look nor taste well (boil
the liver in a separate saucepan). When the water
boils put in a handful of salt, take off the scum as
soon as it rises; have the fish well washed, put it
in, and if it is thick, let it boil very gently. Salmon requires as much boiling as meat; about a
quarter of an hour to a pound of meat; but prac-
tice can only perfect the cook in dressing salmon.

A quarter of a salmon will take as long boiling
as half a one. You must consider the thickness,
not the weight.

3*

Obs. The thinnest part of the fish is the fattest, and if you have a "grand gourmand" at table, ask him if he is for thick or thin.

Lobster sauce and rye bread should be eaten with boiled salmon.

BOILED LOBSTER.

> But soon, like *lobster boil'd*, the morn
> From black to red began to turn.
>   BUTLER.

Those of the middle size are best. The male lobster is preferred to eat, and the female to make sauce of. Set on a pot with water, salted in proportion of a tablespoonful of salt to a quart of water. When the water boils, put it in, and keep it boiling briskly from half an hour to an hour, according to its size; wipe all the scum off it, and rub the shell with a little butter or sweet oil, break off the great claws, crack them carefully in each joint, so that they may not be shattered, and yet come to pieces easily, cut the tail down the middle, and send the body whole.

OYSTERS.

The man had sure a palate cover'd o'er
With brass or steel, that on the rocky shore
First broke the oozy *oyster's* pearly coat,
And risk'd the living morsel down his throat.
                                    GAY.

Common people are indifferent about the manner of opening oysters, and the time of eating them, after they are opened. Nothing, however, is more important in the enlightened eyes of the experienced oyster-eater. Those who wish to enjoy this delicious restorative in its utmost perfection must eat it the moment it is opened, with its own gravy in the under shell. If not eaten while absolutely alive, its flavor and spirit are lost.

FRIED OYSTERS.

You shapeless nothing, in a dish!
You, that are but almost a fish!
                          COWPER.

The largest and finest oysters should be chosen for frying. Simmer them in their own liquor for a couple of minutes; take them out, and lay them on a cloth to drain; beard them, and then flour them, egg and breadcrumb them, put them into boiling fat, and fry them a delicate brown.

A much better way is to beat the yolks of eggs, and mix with the grated bread, a small quantity of beaten nutmeg and mace, and a little salt. Having stirred this batter well, dip your oysters into it, and fry them in lard, till they are a light brown color. Take care not to do them too much. Serve them up hot. For grated bread, some substitute crackers pounded to a powder, and mixed with yolk of egg and spice.

STEWED OYSTERS.

> By nerves about our palate placed,
> She likewise judges of the taste.
> Who would ask for her opinion
> Between an *oyster* and an onion?
> DONNE.

Stew with a quart of oysters, and their liquor strained, a glass of white wine, one anchovy bruised, seasoned with white pepper, salt, a little mace, and a bunch of sweet herbs; let all stew gently an hour, or three quarters. Pick out the bunch of herbs, and add a quarter pound of fresh butter kneaded in a large tablespoonful of flour, and stew them ten or twelve minutes.

Serve them garnished with bread sippets and cut lemon. They may be stewed simply in their own liquor, seasoned with salt, pepper, and grated nutmeg, and thickened with cream, flour, and butter.

OYSTER LOAVES.

'Tis no one thing; it is not fruit, nor root,
Nor poorly limited with head or foot.
DONNE.

Cut off the tops of some small French rolls, take out the crumb, fry them brown and crisp with clarified butter, then fry some breadcrumbs; stew the requisite quantity of oysters, bearded and cut in two, in their liquor, with a little white wine, some gravy, and seasoned with grated lemon-peel, powdered mace, pepper and salt; add a bit of butter, fill the rolls with oysters, and serve them with the fried breadcrumbs in a dish.

SCALLOPED OYSTERS.

What will not luxury taste? Earth, sea, and air,
Are daily ransack'd for the bills of fare.
GAY.

Stew the oysters slowly in their own liquor for two or three minutes, take them out with a spoon, beard them, and skim the liquor, put a bit of but-

ter into a stewpan; when it is melted, add as much
fine breadcrumbs as will dry it up; then put to it
the oyster liquor, and give it a boil up; put the
oysters into scallop shells that you have buttered,
and strewed with breadcrumbs, then a layer of
oysters, then breadcrumbs, and then again oysters;
moisten it with the oyster liquor, cover them with
breadcrumbs, put about half a dozen little bits of
butter on the top of each, and brown them in a
Dutch oven.

Essence of anchovy, ketchup, cayenne, grated
lemon-peel, mace, and other spices are added by
those who prefer piquance to the genuine flavor of
the oyster.

MEATS.

VENISON.

Thanks, my lord, for your *venison;* for finer or fatter
Never ranged in a forest or smoked in a platter.
The haunch was a picture for painters to study,
The fat was so white, and the lean was so ruddy.

GOLDSMITH.

THE haunch of buck will take about three hours
and three quarters roasting. Put a coarse paste
of brown flour and water, and a paper over that,
to cover all the fat; baste it well with dripping,
and keep it at a distance, to get hot at the bones
by degrees. When near done, remove the cover-
ing, and baste it with butter, and froth it up before
you serve. Gravy for it should be put in a boat,
and not in the dish (unless there be none in the
venison), and made thus: cut off the fat from two
or three pounds of a loin of old mutton, and set it
in steaks on a gridiron for a few minutes, just to
brown one side; put them in a saucepan with a
quart of water, cover quite close for an hour, and
gently simmer it; then uncover, and stew till the
gravy be reduced to a pint. Season only with
salt.

VENISON PASTY.

And now that I think on't, as I am a sinner!
We wanted this venison to make out the dinner.
What say you? a *pasty!* it shall and it must,
And my wife, little Kitty, is famous for crust.
" What the de'il, mon, a pasty !" re-echoed the Scot.
" Though splitting, I'll still keep a corner for that."
" We'll all keep a corner," the lady cried out;
" We will all keep a corner !" was echoed about.

GOLDSMITH.

Cut a neck or breast into small steaks, rub them over with a seasoning of sweet herbs, grated nutmeg, pepper and salt; fry them slightly in butter. Line the sides and edges of a dish with puff paste, lay in the steaks, and add half a pint of rich gravy, made with the trimmings of the venison; add a glass of port wine, and the juice of half a lemon or teaspoonful of vinegar; cover the dish with puff paste, and bake it nearly two hours; some more gravy may be poured into the pie before serving it.

ROAST BEEF.

And aye a rowth, a *roast beef* and claret:
Syne wha wad starve !

BURNS.

The noble sirloin of about fifteen pounds will require to be before the fire about three and a half

to four hours; take care to spit it evenly, that it
may not be heavier on one side than on the other;
put a little clean dripping into the dripping-pan
(tie a sheet of paper over to preserve the fat);
baste it well as soon as it is put down, and every
quarter of an hour all the time it is roasting, till
the last half hour; then take off the paper and
make some gravy for it. Stir the fire, and make
it clear; to brown and froth it, sprinkle a little salt
over it, baste it with butter, and dredge it with
flour; let it go a few minutes longer till the froth
rises, take it up, put it on the dish, and serve it.

BEEF À LA BRAISE.

In short, dear, " a Dandy" describes what I mean,
And Bob's far the best of the gems I have seen,
But just knows the names of French dishes and cooks,
As dear Pa knows the titles and authors of books;
Whose names, think how quick! he already knows pat,
A la braise, petit patés, and—what d'ye call that
They inflict on potatoes?   Oh! maître d'hotel.
I assure you, dear Dolly, he knows them as well
As if nothing but these all his life he had eat,
Though a bit of them Bobby has never touched yet.
I can scarce tell the difference, at least as to phrase,
Between *beef à la Psyché* and *curls à la braise.*
                                        MOORE.

Bone a rump of beef, lard it very thickly with
salt pork seasoned with pepper, salt, cloves, mace,

4

and allspice, and season the beef with pepper and
salt; put some slices of bacon into the bottom of
the pan, with some whole black pepper, a little allspice, one or two bay leaves, two onions, a clove
of garlic, and a bunch of sweet herbs. Put in the
beef, and lay over it some slices of bacon, two
quarts of weak stock, and half a pint of white wine.
Cover it closely, and let it stew between six and
seven hours. Sauce for the beef is made of part
of the liquor it has been stewed in, strained, and
thickened with a little flour and butter, adding
some green onions cut small, and pickled mushrooms. Pour it over the beef.

BEEF BAKED WITH POTATOES.

The funeral *bak'd meats*
Did coldly furnish forth the marriage tables.
SHAKSPEARE.

Boil some potatoes, peel, and pound them in a
mortar with two small onions; moisten them with
milk and an egg beaten up, add a little salt and
pepper. Season slices of beef or mutton-chops
with salt and pepper, and more onion, if the flavor
is approved. Rub the bottom of a pudding-dish
with butter, and put a layer of the mashed potatoes, which should be as thick as a batter, and then

a layer of meat, and so on alternately till the dish is filled, ending with potatoes. Bake it in an oven for an hour.

BEEF RAGOUT.

Is there, then, that o'er his *French ragout,*
Looks down wi' sneering, scornful view,
On sic a dinner?
BURNS.

Take a rump of beef, cut the meat from the bone, flour and fry it, pour over it a little boiling water, about a pint of small beer, add a carrot or two, an onion stuck with cloves, some whole pepper, salt, a piece of lemon-peel, a bunch of sweet herbs; let it stew an hour, then add some good gravy; when the meat is tender take it out and strain the sauce; thicken it with a little flour; add a little celery ready boiled, a little ketchup, put in the meat; just simmer it up.

BEEF KIDNEYS.

Or one's *kidney,*—imagine, Dick,—done with champagne.
MOORE.

Having soaked a fresh kidney in cold water and dried it in a cloth, cut it into mouthfuls, and then mince it fine; dust it with flour. Put some butter into a stewpan over a moderate fire, and when it boils put in the minced kidneys. When you have browned it in the butter, sprinkle on a little salt and cayenne, and pour in a very little boiling water. Add a glass of champagne, or other wine, or a large teaspoonful of mushroom ketchup or walnut pickle; cover the pan closely, and let it stew till the kidney is tender. Send it to table hot, in a covered dish. It is eaten generally at breakfast.

BROILED BEEFSTEAKS.

Time was, when John Bull little difference spied
'Twixt the foe at his feet cr the friend at his side;
When he found, such his humor in fighting and eating,
His foe, like *beefsteak*, the sweeter for beating.

MOORE.

If it were done, when 'tis done, then 'twere well,
It were done quickly.

SHAKSPEARE.

Cut the steaks off a rump or the ribs of a fore quarter. Have the gridiron perfectly clean, and heated over a clear quick fire, lay on the steaks, and with meat-tongs, keep turning them constantly, till they are done enough; throw a little salt over them before taking them off the fire. Serve as hot as possible, plain or with a made gravy and sliced onions, or rub a bit of butter on the steaks the moment of serving. Mutton-chops are broiled in the same manner.

SCOTCH HAGGIS.

Fair fa' your honest sonsie face,
Great chieftain o' the puddin' race ;
Aboon them a' ye tak your place,
      Painch, tripe, or thairm,
Weel are ye wordy of a grace
      As langs my arm.
His knife see rustic labor dight,
An' cut you up with ready slight,
Trenching your gushing entrail bright
      Like onie ditch,
And then, O ! what a glorious sight,
      Warm reekin' rich.
Ye powers wha mak mankind your care,
And dish them out their bill of fare,
Auld Scotland wants nae skinking ware
      That jaups in luggies,
But if ye wish her grateful pray'r,
      Gie her a *Haggis*.
                    BURNS.

Make the haggis bag perfectly clean; parboil the draught, boil the liver very well, so as it will grate, dry the meal before the fire, mince the draught and a pretty large piece of beef, very

4*

small ; grate about half the liver, mince plenty of
the suet and some onions small ; mix all these ma-
terials very well together with a handful or two
of the dried meal ; spread them on the table, and
season them properly with salt and mixed spices ;
take any of the scraps of beef that are left from
mincing, and some of the water that boiled the
draught, and make about a choppin (*i. e.* a quart)
of good stock of it ; then put all the haggis meat
into the bag, and that broth in it ; then sew up
the bag ; put out all the wind before you sew it
quite close.   If you think the bag is thin, you may
put it in a cloth.

If it is a large haggis, it will take at least two
hours boiling.

N. B. The above is a receipt from Mrs. MacIver,
a celebrated Caledonian professor of the culinary
art, who taught and published a book of cookery,
at Edinburgh, A. D. 1787.

SALT BEEF.

The British fleet, which now commands the main,
Might glorious wreaths of victory obtain,
Would they take time, would they with leisure work,
With care would *salt their beef,* and cure their pork.
There is no dish, but what *our* cooks have made
And merited a charter by their trade.

                                KING.

Make a pickle of rock salt and cold water strong

enough to bear an egg, let a little salt remain in the bottom of the tub; two quarts of molasses and a quarter pound of saltpetre is sufficient for a cwt. of beef. It is fit for use in ten days. Boil the beef slowly until the bones come out easily, then wrap it in a towel, and put a heavy weight on it till cold.

TO PICKLE TONGUES FOR BOILING.

Silence is commendable only
In a *neat's tongue* dried.
SHAKSPEARE.

Cut off the root, leaving a little of the kernel and fat. Sprinkle some salt, and let it drain till next day; then for each tongue, mix a large spoonful of common salt, the same of coarse sugar, and about half as much of saltpetre; rub it well in, and do so every day. In a week add another heaped spoonful of salt. If rubbed every day, a tongue will be ready in a fortnight; but if only turned in the pickle daily, it will keep four or five weeks without being too salt. Smoke them or plainly dry them, if you like best. When to be dressed, boil it extremely tender; allow five hours, and if done sooner, it is easily kept hot. The longer kept after drying, the higher it will be; if hard, it may require soaking three or four hours.

ROASTED CALF'S LIVER.

Pray a slice of your *liver*.
GOLDSMITH.

Wash and wipe it, then cut a long hole in it, and stuff it with crumbs of bread, chopped, an anchovy, a good deal of fat bacon, onion, salt, pepper, a bit of butter, and an egg; stew the liver up, lard it, wrap it in a veal caul, and roast it. Serve with good brown gravy and currant jelly.

SCOTCH COLLOPS.

A cook has mighty things professed;
Then send us but two dishes nicely dressed,—
One called *Scotch Collops*.
KING.

Cut veal in thin bits, about three inches over and rather round, beat with a rolling-pin; grate a little nutmeg over them; dip in the yolk of an egg, and fry them in a little butter of a fine brown; have ready, warm, to pour upon them, half a pint of gravy, a little bit of butter rubbed into a little flour, to which put the yolk of an egg, two large spoonfuls of cream, and a little salt.

Do not boil the sauce, but stir until of a fine thickness to serve with the collops.

STEWED FILLET OF VEAL.

In truth, I'm confounded
And bothered, my dear, 'twixt that troublesome boy's
(Bob's) cookery language, and Madame Le Roi's.
What with fillets of roses and *fillets of veal*,
Things garni with lace, and things garni with eel,
One's hair and one's cutlets both en papillote,
And a thousand more things I shall ne'er have by rote.

MOORE.

Bone, lard, and stuff a fillet of veal; half roast and then stew it with two quarts of white stock, a teaspoonful of lemon pickle, and one of mushroom ketchup. Before serving strain the gravy, thicken it with butter rolled in flour, add a little cayenne, salt, and some pickled mushrooms; heat it and pour it over the veal. Have ready two or three dozen forcemeat balls to put round it and upon the top. Garnish with cut lemon.

CALF'S HEAD SURPRISED.

And the dish set before them,—O dish well devised!—
Was what Old Mother Glasse calls "*a calf's head surprised.*"

MOORE.

Clean and blanch a calf's head, boil it till the bones will come out easily, then bone and press it between two dishes, so as to give it a headlong form; beat it with the yolks of four eggs, a little melted butter, pepper and salt. Divide the head when cold, and brush it all over with the beaten eggs, and strew over it grated bread, which is put over one half; a good quantity of finely minced parsley should be mixed; place the head upon a dish, and bake it of a nice brown color. Serve it with a sauce of parsley and butter, and with one of good gravy, mixed with the brains, which have been previously boiled, chopped, and seasoned with a little cayenne and salt.

CALF'S HEAD ROASTED.

Good L—d! to see the various ways
Of dressing a calf's head.
SHENSTONE.

Wash and clean it well, parboil it, take out the bones, brains, and tongue; make forcemeat sufficient for the head, and some balls with bread-crumbs, minced suet, parsley, grated ham, and a little pounded veal or cold fowl; season with salt, grated nutmeg, and lemon-peel; bind it with an egg beaten up; fill the head with it, which must then be sewed up, or fastened with skewers and tied; while roasting baste it well with butter; beat up the brains with a little cream, the yolk of an egg, some minced parsley, a little pepper and salt;

blanch the tongue and cut it into slices, and fry it
with the brains, forcemeat balls, and thin slices of
bacon.

Serve the head with white or brown thickened
gravy, and place the tongue and forcemeat balls
round it. Garnish with cut lemon. It will require
one hour and a half to roast.

SALMIS OF WILD DUCK.

Long as, by bayonets protected, we Watties
May have our full fling at their *salmis* and patés.
                                        MOORE.

Cut off the best parts of a couple of roasted wild
ducks, and put the rest of the meat into a mortar,
with six shallots, a little parsley, some pepper,
and a bay leaf; pound all these ingredients well,
and then put into a saucepan, with four ladlesful
of stock, half a glass of white wine, the same of
broth, and a little grated nutmeg; reduce these to
half, strain them, and having laid the pieces on a
dish, cover them with the above; keep the whole
hot, not boiling, until wanted for table.

STEWED DUCK AND PEAS.

I give thee all my kitchen lore,
    Though poor the offering be;
I'll tell thee how 'tis cooked, before
    You come to dine with me.
The duck is truss'd from head to heels,
    Then stew'd with butter well,
And streaky bacon, which reveals
    A most delicious smell.

When duck and bacon, in a mass,
    You in a stewpan lay,
A spoon around the vessel pass,
    And gently stir away;
A tablespoonful of flour bring,
    A quart of water plain,
Then in it twenty onions fling,
    And gently stir again.

A bunch of parsley, and a leaf
    Of ever verdant bay,
Two cloves,—I make my language brief,—
    Then add your peas you may;
And let it simmer till it sings
    In a delicious strain;
Then take your duck, nor let the strings
    For trussing it remain.

The parsley fail not to remove,
    Also the leaf of bay;
Dish up your duck,—the sauce improve
    In the accustom'd way,
With pepper, salt, and other things
    I need not here explain;
And if the dish contentment brings,
    You'll dine with me again.

FOWL À LA HOLLANDAISE.

Our courtier walks from dish to dish,
Tastes from his friends of *fowl* and fish,
Tells all their names, lays down the law,
" Que ça est bon." " Ah! goutez ça."
                    POPE.

Make a forcemeat of grated bread, half its quantity of minced suet, an onion, or a few oysters and some boiled parsley, season with pepper, salt, and grated lemon-peel, and an egg beaten up to bind it. Bone the breast of a good sized young fowl, put in the forcemeat, cover the fowl with a piece of white paper buttered, and roast it half an hour; make a thick batter of flour, milk, and eggs, take off the paper, and pour some of the batter over the fowl; as soon as it becomes dry, add more, and do this till it is all crusted over and a nice brown color, serve it with melted butter and lemon pickle, or a thickened brown gravy.

BOILED TURKEY.

But man, cursed man, on *turkeys* preys,
And Christmas shortens all our days.
Sometimes with oysters we combine,
Sometimes assist the savory chine.
From the low peasant to the lord,
The *turkey* smokes on every board.

GAY.

Make a stuffing of bread, salt, pepper, nutmeg,
lemon-peel, a few oysters, a bit of butter, some
suet, and an egg; put this into the crop, fasten up
the skin, and boil the turkey in a floured cloth to
make it very white. Have ready some oyster
sauce made rich with butter, a little cream, and a
spoonful of soy, and serve over the turkey.

DEVILLED TURKEY.

And something's here with name uncivil,
For our cook christens it "*A Devil,*"
"*A Devil,* in any shape, sweet maid,
A parson fears not," Syntax said;
"I'll make him minced meat; 'tis my trade."

Take cold roast turkey legs, score them well,
season them with salt and plenty of cayenne pepper and mustard, then broil them. Serve them
hot.

CAPON.

In good roast beef my landlord sticks his knife,
The *capon* fat delights his dainty wife.

GAY.

Take a quart of white wine, season the capon
with salt, cloves, and whole pepper, a few shallots,
and then put the capon in an earthen pan; you
must take care it has not room to shake; it must
be covered close, and done over a slow charcoal
fire.

CHICKEN CROQUETTES.

Gargilius, sleek, voluptuous lord,
A hundred dainties smoke upon his board;
Earth, air, and ocean ransack'd for the feast,
In masquerade of foreign olios dress'd.

WARTON.

Reduce two spoonfuls of veloute or sauce tournée,
and add to the yolks of four eggs; put to this the
white meat of a chicken, minced very small, and
well mixed with the sauce; take it out, and roll it
into balls, about the size of a walnut; roll them
in breadcrumbs, giving them an elongated form;
then beat them in some well-beaten egg; bread
them again, and fry them of a light brown.

LEG OF MUTTON.

But hang it, to poets, who seldom can eat,
Your very good *mutton's* a very good treat.
GOLDSMITH.

Cut off the shank bone, and trim the knuckle, put it into lukewarm water for ten minutes, wash it clean, cover it with cold water, and let it simmer very gently, and skim it carefully; a leg of nine pounds will take two and a half or three hours, if you like it thoroughly done, especially in very cold weather.

The liquor the mutton is boiled in, you may convert into good soup in five minutes, and Scotch barley broth. Thus managed, a leg of mutton is a most economical joint.

TO CURE HAMS.

Or urged thereunto by the woes he endured,
The way to be *smoked*, is the way to be *cured*.
ANONYMOUS.

But to the fading palate bring relief,
By the *Westphalian ham* or Belgic beef.
KING.

When the weather will permit, hang the ham three days; mix an ounce of saltpetre with one quarter of a pound of bay salt, ditto common salt, ditto of coarsest sugar, and a quart of strong beer; boil them together, and pour over immediately on the ham; turn it twice a day in the pickle for three weeks. An ounce of black pepper, ditto of pimento in finest powder, added to the above, will give still more flavor. Cover with bran when wiped, and smoke from three to four weeks, as you approve; the latter will make it harder, and more of the flavor of Westphalia. Sew hams in hessings, *i. e.* coarse wrapper, if to be smoked where there is a strong fire.

HAM PIES.

Each mortal has his pleasure; none deny
Scarsdale his bottle, Darby his *ham pie.*
DODSLEY.

Take two pounds of veal cutlets, cut them in middling sized pieces, season with pepper and a very little salt; likewise one of raw or dressed ham, cut in slices, lay it alternately in the dish, and put some forced or sausage meat at the top, with some stewed mushrooms, and the yolks of three eggs boiled hard, and a gill of water; then proceed as with rumpsteak pie.

N. B. The best end of a neck is the fine part for a pie, cut into chops, and the chine bone taken away.

ROASTED HARE.

Turkey and fowl, and ham and chine,
On which the cits prefer to dine,
With partridge, too, and eke a *Hare*,
The luxuries of country fare,
She nicely cooked with bounteous care.

Cut the skin from a hare that has been well
soaked, put it on the spit, and rub it well with
Madeira, pricking it in various places that it may
imbibe plenty of wine; cover it entirely with a
paste, and roast it. When done, take away the
paste, rub it quickly over with egg, sprinkle breadcrumbs, and baste it gently with butter (still keeping it turning before the fire), until a crust is
formed over it, and it is of a nice brown color;
dish it over some espagnole with Madeira wine
boiled in it; two or three cloves may be stuck into
the knuckles, if you think proper.

FRICASEED RABBITS.

Your *rabbits fricaseed* and chicken,
With curious choice of dainty picking,
Each night got ready at the Crown,
With port and punch to wash 'em down.
                              LLOYD.

Take two fine white rabbits, and cut them in
pieces; blanch them in boiling water, and skim

them for one minute; stir a few trimmings of mushrooms in a stewpan over the fire, with a bit of
butter, till it begins to fry, then stir in a spoonful
of flour; mix into the flour, a little at a time,
nearly a quart of good consommé, which set on
the fire, and when it boils put the rabbits in, and
let them boil gently till done; then put them in
another stewpan, and reduce the sauce till nearly
as thick as paste; mix in about half a pint of good
boiling cream, and when it becomes the thickness
of bechamelle sauce in general, squeeze it through
the tammy to the rabbits; make it very hot, put in
a few mushrooms, the yolk of an egg, a little cream,
and then serve it to table.

BIRDS.

TO ROAST PHEASANTS.

Little birds fly about with the *true pheasant taint,*
And the geese are all born with the liver* complaint.
MOORE.

Chop some fine raw oysters, omitting the head part, mix them with salt and nutmeg, and add some beaten yolk of egg to bind the other ingredients. Cut some very thin slices of cold ham or bacon, and cover the birds with them, then wrap them in sheets of paper well buttered, put them on the spit, and roast them before a clear fire.

TO ROAST ORTOLANS.

With all the luxury of statesmen dine,
On daily feasts of *ortolans* and wine.
CAWTHORN.

Put into every bird an oyster, or a little butter

---

* The process by which the liver of the unfortunate goose is enlarged, in order to produce that richest of all dainties, *the foie gras,* of which such renowned pâtés are made at Strasbourg and Toulouse, is thus described in the "Cours Gastronomique:" "On deplumes l'estomac des oies; on attache ensuite ces animaux aux chenets d'une cheminée, et on le nourrit devant le feu. La captivité et la chaleur donnent a ces volatiles une maladie hepatique, qui fait gonfler leur foie.'

mixed with some finely sifted breadcrumbs. Dredge them with flour. Run a small skewer through them, and tie them on the spit. Baste them with lard or fresh butter. They will be done in ten minutes. Reed birds are very fine made into little dumplings with a thin crust of flour and butter, and boiled about twenty minutes. Each must be tied in a separate cloth.

WOODCOCKS.

And as for your juries—who would not set o'er them
A jury of tasters, with *woodcocks* before them?

MOORE.

Woodcocks should not be drawn, as the trail is by the lovers of "haut gout" considered a "bonne bouche." Truss their legs close to the body, and run an iron skewer through each thigh, and put them to roast before the fire; toast a slice of bread for each bird, lay them in the dripping-pan under the bird to catch the trail; baste them with butter, and froth them with flour; lay the toast on a hot dish, and the birds on the toast; pour some good beef gravy into the dish, and send some up in a boat. Twenty or thirty minutes will roast them. Some epicures like this bird very much underdone, and direct that the woodcock should be just introduced to the cook, for her to show it to the fire, then send it to table.

BIRDS POTTED.

"It tastes of the *bird*, however," said the old woman, "and she cooked the *rail of the fence* on which the crow had been sitting."

When birds have come a great way, they often smell so bad that they can scarcely be borne from the rankness of the butter, by managing them in the following manner, they may be as good as ever. Set a large saucepan of clean water on the fire, when it boils take off the butter at the top, then take the fowls out one by one, throw them in the saucepan of water half a minute, whip it out, and dry it in a cloth inside and out, continue till they are all done; scald the pot clean, when the birds are quite cold, season them with mace, pepper, and salt according to taste, put them down close in a pot, and pour clarified butter over them.

LARKS.

What say you, lads? is any spark
Among you ready for a *lark?*
                    MOORE.

These delicate little birds are in high season in November. When they are thoroughly picked, gutted, and cleansed, truss them; do them over with the yolk of an egg, and then roll them in breadcrumbs; spit them on a lark spit; ten or fifteen minutes will be sufficient time to roast them in, before a quick fire; whilst they are roasting, baste them with fresh butter, and sprinkle them with breadcrumbs till they are well covered with them. Fry some grated bread in butter. Set it to drain before the fire, that it may harden; serve the crumbs in the dish under the larks, and garnish with slices of lemon.

MISCELLANEOUS.

STUFFING FOR VEAL.

Poor Roger Fowler, who'd a generous mind,
Nor would submit to have his hand confined,
But aimed at all,—yet never could excel
In anything but *stuffing of his veal.*

Good stuffing has always been considered a chief
thing in cookery.   Mince a quarter of a pound of
beef suet or marrow, the same weight of breadcrumbs, two drachms of parsley leaves, a drachm
and a half of sweet marjoram or lemon thyme, and
the same of grated lemon-peel and onion chopped
as fine as possible, a little pepper and salt; pound
thoroughly together with the yolk and white of
two eggs, and secure it in the veal with a skewer,
or sew it in with a bit of thread.

FORCEMEAT BALLS.

And own they gave him a lively notion,
What his own *forced meat balls* would be.
MOORE.

Take an equal quantity of lean veal scraped, and
beef suet shred, beat them in a marble mortar, add

pepper, salt, cloves, pounded lemon-peel, and nutmeg grated, parsley, and sweet herbs chopped fine, a little shallot and young onion, a few breadcrumbs grated fine, and yolk of egg, sufficient to work it light; roll this into balls with a little flour, and fry them.

VOL AU VENT.

Boy, tell the cook I love all nicknackeries,
Fricasees, *vol au vents*, puffs, and gimcrackeries.
MOORE.

Roll off tart paste till about the eighth of an inch thick, then with a tin cutter made for that purpose cut out the shape (about the size of the bottom of the dish you intend sending to table), lay it on a baking-plate with paper, rub the paste over with the yolk of an egg. Roll out good puff paste an inch thick, stamp it with the same cutter, and lay it on the tart paste; then take a cutter two sizes smaller, and press it in the centre nearly through the puff paste; rub the top with yolk of egg, and bake it in a quick oven about twenty minutes, of a light-brown color when done; take out the paste inside the centre mark, preserving the top, put it on a dish in a warm place, and when wanted fill it with a white fricasee of chicken, rabbit, ragout of sweetbread, or any other entree you wish. Serve hot.

OYSTER PATTIE.

De Beringhen. In the next room there's a delicious pâté, let's discuss it.

Baradas. Pshaw! a man filled with a sublime ambition has no time to discuss your pâtés.

De Beringhen. Pshaw! and a man filled with as sublime a pâté has no time to discuss ambition. Gad, I have the best of it.

BULWER'S RICHELIEU.

Beard a quart of fine oysters, strain the liquor and add them to it. Cut into thin slices the kidney-fat of a loin of veal; season them with white pepper, salt, mace, and grated lemon-peel; lay them on the bottom of a pie-dish, put in the oysters and liquor, with a little more seasoning; put over them the marrow of two bones. Lay a border of puff paste around the edge of the dish, cover it with paste, and bake it nearly three quarters of an hour.

PATTIES FOR FRIED BREAD.

Seducing young pâtés, as ever could cozen
One out of one's appetite, down by the dozen.
MOORE.

Cut the crumb of a loaf of bread into square or round pieces, nearly three inches high, and cut bits the same width for tops. Mark them neatly with a knife; fry the bread of a light-brown color in clarified beef-dripping or fine lard; scoop out the inside crumb; take care not to go too near the bottom; fill them with mince-meat prepared as for patties, with stewed oysters or with sausage meat; put on the tops, and serve them on a napkin.

MACARONI GRATIN.

Where so ready all nature its cookery yields,
Macaroni au Parmesan grows in the fields.
MOORE.

Lay fried bread pretty closely round a dish; boil your macaroni in the usual way, and pour it into the dish; smooth it all over, and strew bread-crumbs on it, then a pretty thick layer of grated Parmesan cheese; drop a little melted butter on it, and put it in the oven to brown.

TRUFFLES.

What will not *Luxury taste?* *Earth*, sea and air
Are daily ransacked for the bill of fare.
GAY.

The truffle, like the mushroom, is a species of fungus, common in France and Italy; it is generally about eight to ten inches below the surface of the ground.   As it imparts a most delicious flavor, it is much used in cookery.

Being dug out of the earth, it requires a great deal of washing and brushing.   It loses much of its flavor when dried.

TO STEW MUSHROOMS.

Muse, sing the man that did to Paris go,
That he might taste their soups and *mushrooms* know.
KING.

Take a pint of white stock; season it with salt, pepper, and a little lemon pickle, thicken it with a bit of butter rolled in flour; clean and peel the mushrooms, sprinkle them with a very little salt, boil them for three minutes; put them into the gravy when it is hot, and stew them for fifteen minutes.

SAUCES.

MUSHROOM KETCHUP.

If you please,
I'll taste your tempting toasted cheese,
Broiled ham, and nice *mushroom'd ketchup*.

If you love good ketchup, gentle reader, make it yourself, after the following directions, and you will have a delicious relish for made dishes, ragouts, soup, sauces, or hashes. Mushroom gravy approaches the nature and flavor of made gravy, more than any vegetable juice, and is the superlative substitute for it; in meagre soups and extempore gravies, the chemistry of the kitchen has yet contrived to agreeably awaken the palate and encourage the appetite.

A couple quarts of double ketchup, made according to the following receipt, will save you some score pounds of meat, besides a vast deal of time and trouble, as it will furnish, in a few minutes, as good sauce as can be made for either fish, flesh, or fowl. I believe the following is the best way for preparing and extracting the essence of mushrooms, so as to procure and preserve their flavor for a considerable length of time.

Look out for mushrooms, from the beginning of September. Take care of the right sort and fresh gathered. Full-grown flaps are to be preferred. Put a layer of these at the bottom of a deep earthen pan, and sprinkle them with salt; then another layer of mushrooms, and some more salt on them, and so on, alternately, salt and mushrooms; let them remain two or three hours, by which time the salt will have penetrated the mushrooms, and rendered them easy to break; then pound them in a mortar, or mash them well with your hands, and let them remain for a couple of days, not longer, stirring them up, and mashing them well each day; then pour them into a stone jar, and to each quart add an ounce and a half of whole black pepper, and half an ounce of allspice; stop the jar very close, and set in a stewpan of boiling water, and keep it boiling for two hours at least.

Take out the jar, and pour the juice, clear from the settlings, through a hair sieve (without squeezing the mushrooms), into a clean stewpan; let it boil very gently for half an hour. Those who are for superlative ketchup, will continue the boiling till the mushroom juice is reduced to half the quantity. There are several advantages attending this concentration: it will keep much better, and only half

the quantity required; so you can flavor sauce,
&c., without thinning it; neither is this an extra-
vagant way of making it, for merely the aqueous
part is evaporated. Skim it well, and pour it into
a clean dry jar or jug; cover it close, and let it
stand in a cool place till next day; then pour it
off as gently as possible (so as not to disturb the
settlings at the bottom of the jug), through a tamis
or thick flannel bag, till it is perfectly clear; add
a tablespoonful of good brandy to each pint of ketchup, and let it stand as before; a fresh sediment
will be deposited, from which the ketchup is to be
quietly poured off and bottled in pints or half pints
(which have been washed in brandy or spirits). It
is best to keep it in such quantities as are soon
used.

Take especial care that it is closely corked and
sealed down. If kept in a cool dry place, it may
be preserved for a long time; but if it be badly
corked, and kept in a damp place, it will soon
spoil.

Examine it from time to time, by placing a
strong light behind the neck of the bottle, and if
any pellicle appears about it, boil it up again with
a few peppercorns.

SUPERLATIVE SAUCE.

Who praises, in this *sauce enamor'd* age,
Calm, healthful temperance, like an Indian sage?

WARTON.

Claret or Port wine and mushroom ketchup, a pint of each; half a pint of walnut or other pickle liquor; pounded anchovies, four ounces; fresh lemon-peel, pared very thin, an ounce; peeled and sliced eschalots, the same; scraped horse-radish, ditto; allspice and black pepper, powdered, half an ounce each; cayenne, one drachm, or curry powder, three drachms; celery seed, bruised, one drachm; all avoirdupois weight. Put these into a wide-mouthed bottle, stop it close, shake it every day for a fortnight, and strain it (when some think it improved by the addition of a quarter of a pint of soy or thick browning), and you will have "a delicious double relish." Dr. Kitchener says, this composition is one of the chefs d'œuvres of many experiments he has made, for the purpose of enabling good housewives to prepare their own sauces; it is equally agreeable with fish, game, poultry, or ragouts, &c.; and as a fair lady may make it herself, its relish will be not a little aug-mented, that all the ingredients are good and wholesome.

Obs. Under an infinity of circumstances, a cook

may be in want of the substances necessary to make sauce ; the above composition of the several articles from which the various gravies derive their flavor, will be found a very admirable extemporaneous substitute. By mixing a large tablespoonful with a quarter of a pint of thickened melted butter, or broth, five minutes will finish a boat of very relishing sauce, nearly equal to drawn gravy, and as likely to put your lingual nerves into good humor as anything I know.

MINT SAUCE.

"Live bullion," says merciless Bob, " which I think
Would, if coined with a little *mint sauce*, be delicious."
MOORE.

Wash half a handful of nice, young, fresh-gathered green mint (to this add one-third the quantity of parsley), pick the leaves from the stalks, mince them very fine, and put them into a sauceboat, with a teaspoonful of moist sugar and four tablespoonfuls of vinegar.

CRANBERRY SAUCE.

Our fathers most admired their sauces sweet,
And often asked for sugar with their meat.

KING.

Wash a quart of ripe cranberries, and put them into a pan with just about a teacup of water; stew them slowly and stir them frequently, particularly after they begin to burst. They require a great deal of stewing, and should be like marmalade when done. When they are broken and the juice comes out, stir in a pound of white sugar. When they are thoroughly done, put them into a deep dish, and set them away to get cold. You may strain the pulp through a cullender or sieve into a mould, and when it is a firm shape send it to table.

Cranberry sauce is eaten with roast fowl, turkey, &c.

CAPER SAUCE.

Along these shores
Neglected trade with difficulty toils,
Collecting slender stores; the sun-dried grape,
Or *capers* from the rock, that prompt the taste
Of luxury.

DYER.

To make a quarter of a pint, take a tablespoonful of capers and two teaspoonfuls of vinegar.

The present fashion of cutting capers is to mince one-third of them very fine, and divide the others in half; put them into a quarter of a pint of melted butter, or good thickened gravy; stir them the same way as you did the melted butter, or it will oil. Some boil and mince fine a few leaves of parsley or chevrel or tarragon, and add to the sauce; others, the juice of half a Seville orange or lemon.

VEGETABLES.

Grateful and salutary Spring! the *plants*
Which crown thy numerous gardens, and invite
To health and temperance, in the simple meal,
Unstain'd with murder, undefil'd with blood,
Unpoison'd with rich sauces, to provoke
The unwilling appetite to gluttony.
For this, the *bulbous esculents* their roots
With sweetness fill; for this, with cooling juice
The green herb spreads its *leaves;* and opening *buds*
And *flowers* and *seeds* with various flavors tempts
Th' ensanguined palate from its savage feast.

DODSLEY.

As to the quality of vegetables, the middle size are preferred to the largest or smallest; they are more tender, juicy, and full of flavor, just before they are quite full grown. Freshness is their chief value and excellence, and I should as soon think of roasting an animal alive, as of boiling a vegetable after it is dead.

To boil them in soft water will preserve the color best of such as are green; if you have only hard water, put to it a teaspoonful of carbonate of potash.

Take care to wash and cleanse them thoroughly from dust, dirt, and insects. This requires great attention.

If you wish to have vegetables delicately clean, put on your pot, make it boil, put a little salt in it, and skim it perfectly clean before you put in the greens, &c., which should not be put in till the water boils briskly; the quicker they boil, the greener they will be. When the vegetables sink, they are generally done enough, if the water has been kept constantly boiling. Take them up immediately, or they will lose their color and goodness. Drain the water from them thoroughly before you send them to table.

This branch of cookery requires the most vigilant attention.

TO DRESS SALAD.

Two large potatoes, pressed through kitchen sieve,
Smoothness and softness to the *salad* give;
Of mordant mustard add a single spoon;
Distrust the condiment that bites too soon;
But deem it not, thou man of herbs, a fault,
To add a double quantity of salt.
Four times the spoon with oil of Lucca crown,
And twice with vinegar procured from town;
True flavor needs it, and your poet begs
The pounded yellow of two boiled eggs;
Let onion's atoms lurk within the bowl,
And, scarce suspected, animate the whole;

And, lastly, in the flavored compound toss
A magic spoonful of anchovy sauce.
O great and glorious! O herbaceous treat!
'Twould tempt the dying anchorite to eat,
Back to the world he'd turn his weary soul,
And plunge his fingers in the salad bowl.

REV. SIDNEY SMITH.

If the herbs be young, fresh-gathered, trimmed neatly, and drained dry and the sauce-maker ponders patiently over the above directions, he cannot fail of obtaining the fame of being a very accomplished salad-dresser.

ONIONS.

The things we eat, by various juice control
The narrowness or largeness of our soul.
Onions will make e'en heirs or widows weep;
The tender lettuce brings on softer sleep.

KING

Peel a pint of button onions, and put them in water till you want to put them on to boil; put them into a stewpan, with a quart of cold water; let them boil till tender; they will take (according to their size and age) from half an hour to an hour.

ARTICHOKES.

Whose appetites would soon devour
Each cabbage, *artichoke*, and flower.
CAWTHORNE.

Soak them in cold water, wash them well, then put them into plenty of boiling water, with a handful of salt, and let them boil gently till tender, which will take an hour and a half or two hours. The surest way to know when they are done enough is to draw out a leaf. Trim them and drain them on a sieve, and send up melted butter with them, which some put into small cups, so that each guest may have one.

LIMA BEANS.

Now fragrant with the *bean's* perfume,
Now purpled with the pulse's bloom,
Might well with bright allusions store me;
But happier bards have been before me.
SHENSTONE.

These are generally considered the finest of all beans, and should be gathered young. Shell them, lay them in a pan of cold water, and then boil them about two hours, or till they are quite soft; drain them well, and add to them some butter. They are destroyed by the first frost, but can be kept during the winter by gathering them on a dry day, when full grown, but not the least hard, and putting them in their pods into a keg. Throw some salt into the bottom of the keg, and cover it with a layer of bean pods, then add more salt, and then another layer of beans in their pods, till the keg is full. Press them down with a heavy weight, cover the keg closely, and keep it in a cool, dry place. Before you use them, soak the pods all night in cold water, the next day shell them, and soak the beans till you are ready to boil them.

POTATOES.

Leeks to the Welsh, to Dutchmen butter's dear;
Of Irish swains, *potatoes* is the cheer.
GAY.

Wash them, but do not pare or cut them, unless they are very large. Fill a saucepan half full of potatoes of equal size (or make them so by dividing the larger ones), put to them as much cold water as will cover them about an inch; they are sooner boiled, and more savory than when drowned in water. Most boiled things are spoiled by having too little water; but potatoes are often spoiled by having too much; they must be merely covered, and a little allowed for waste in boiling, so that they may be just covered at the finish. Set them on a moderate fire till they boil; then take them off, and put them by the side of the fire to simmer slowly till they are soft enough to admit a fork. Place no dependence on the usual test of their skins cracking, which, if they are boiled fast, will happen to some potatoes when they are not half done, and the insides quite hard. Then pour the water off—(if you let the potatoes remain in the water a moment after they are done enough, they will become waxy and watery),—uncover the soucepan, and set it at such a distance from the fire as will secure it from burning; their superfluous moisture will evaporate, and the potatoes will be perfectly dry and mealy.

You may afterwards place a napkin, folded up to the size of the saucepan's diameter, over the potatoes, to keep them hot and mealy till wanted.

This method of managing potatoes is in every respect equal to steaming them, and they are dressed in half the time.

There is such an infinite variety of sorts and sizes of potatoes, it is impossible to say how long they will take doing: the best way is to try them with a fork. Moderate sized potatoes will generally be done enough in fifteen or twenty minutes.

PEAS.

Your infant *peas* to asparagus prefer;
Which to the supper you may best defer.

KING.

Young green peas, well dressed, are among the most delicious delicacies of the vegetable kingdom. They must be young. It is equally indispensable that they be fresh gathered, and cooked as soon as they are shelled, for they soon lose both their color and sweetness. After being shelled, wash them, drain them in a cullender, put them on, in plenty of boiling water, with a teaspoonful of salt; boil them till they become tender, which, if young, will be less than half an hour; if old, they will require more than an hour. Drain them in a cullender, and put them into a dish, with a slice of fresh butter in it. Some people think it an improvement to boil a small bunch of mint with the peas; it is then minced finely, and laid in small heaps at the end or sides of the dish. If peas are allowed to stand in the water, after being boiled, they lose their color.

RICE.

Every week dispense
English beans or *Carolinian rice.*

GRAINGER.

Wash the rice perfectly clean; put on one pound
in two quarts of cold water; let it boil twenty minutes; strain it through a sieve, and put it before
the fire; shake it up with a fork every now and
then, to separate the grains, and make it quite dry.
Serve it hot.

TURNIPS.

On *turnips* feast whene'er you please,
And riot in my beans and peas.

GAY.

Wash, peel, and boil them till tender, in water
with a little salt; serve them with melted butter.
Or they may be stewed in a pint of milk, thickened
with a bit of butter rolled in flour, and seasoned
with salt and pepper, and served with the sauce.

SPINACH.

Much meat doth Gluttony procure,
To feed men fat as swine;
But he's a frugal man, indeed,
That on *the leaf* can dine.

Pick it very carefully, and wash it thoroughly

two or three times; then put it on in boiling water
with a little salt; let it boil nearly twenty minutes.
Put it into a cullender; hold it under the water-
cock, and let the water run on it for a minute.   Put
it into a saucepan; beat it perfectly smooth with a
wooden spoon; add a bit of butter, and three tablespoonfuls of cream.   Mix it well together, and
make it hot before serving.

ASPARAGUS.

At early morn, I to the market haste,
(Studious in everything to please thy taste);
A curious fowl and *'sparagus* I chose,
(For I remembered you were fond of those).
GAY.

Boil asparagus in salt and water till it is tender
at the stalk, which will be in twenty or thirty minutes.   Great care must be taken to watch the
exact time of its becoming tender.   Toast some
bread; dip it lightly in the liquor the asparagus
was boiled in, and lay it in the middle of the dish;
melt some butter; lay the asparagus upon the
toast, which must project beyond the asparagus,
that the company may see that there is toast.

CARROTS.

And when his juicy salads fail'd,
Slic'd *carrots* pleased him well.
                                    COWPER.

Let them be well washed and brushed, not scraped. If young spring carrots, an hour is enough. When done, rub off the peels with a clean coarse cloth, and slice them in two or four, according to their size. The best way to try if they are boiled enough, is to pierce them with a fork.

LEEKS.

With carrots red, and turnips white,
And *leeks*, Cadwallader's delight,
And all the savory crop that vie
To please the palate and the eye.
                                    GRAINGER.

Leeks are most generally used for soups, ragouts, and other made dishes. They are very rarely brought to table; in which case dress them as follows. Put them in the stock pot till about three parts done; then take them out, drain and soak them in vinegar seasoned with pepper, salt, and cloves; drain them again, stuff their hearts with a farce, dip them in butter, and fry them.

TO DRY HERBS.

Herbs too she knew, and well of each could speak
 That in her garden sipp'd the silvery dew,
Where no vain flower disclosed a gaudy streak,
 But herbs, for use and physic, not a few
Of gray renown, within those borders grew,—
 The *tufted basil, pun-provoking thyme,*
Fresh *balm,* and *marigold* of cheerful hue,
 The *lowly gill,* that never dares to climb,
And more I fain would sing, disdaining here to rhyme.
         Shenstone.

It is very important to know when the various seasons commence for picking sweet and savory herbs for drying. Care should be taken that they are gathered on a dry day, by which means they will have a better color when dried. Cleanse them well from dirt and dust, cut off the roots, separate the bunches into smaller ones, and dry them by the heat of the stove, or in a Dutch oven before a common fire, in such quantities at a time, that the process may be speedily finished, *i. e.* "Kill 'em quick," says a great botanist; by this means their flavor will be best preserved. There can be no doubt of the propriety of drying, &c., hastily by the aid

of artificial heat, rather than by the heat of the
sun. In the application of artificial heat, the only
caution requisite is to avoid burning; and of this
a sufficient test is afforded by the preservation of
the color. The best method to preserve the flavor
of aromatic plants is to pick off the leaves as soon
as they are dried, and to pound them, and put
them through a hair sieve, and keep them in well-
stopped bottles labelled.

PICKLES.

MANGOES.

What lord of old would bid his cook prepare
Mangoes, potargo, champignons, caviare !
KING.

There is a particular sort of melon for this purpose. Cut a square small piece out of one side, and through that take out the seeds, mix with them mustard seeds and shred garlic, stuff the melon as full as the space will allow, and replace the square piece. Bind it up with small new packthread. Boil a good quantity of vinegar, to allow for wasting, with peppers, salt, ginger, and pour it boiling over the mangoes, four successive days; the last day put flour of mustard and scraped horseradish into the vinegar just as it boils up. Observe that there is plenty of vinegar. All pickles are spoiled, if not well covered.

PICKLED CABBAGE.

Lives in a cell, and eats from week to week
A meal of *pickled cabbage* and ox cheek.

CAWTHORNE.

Choose two middling-sized, well-colored and firm red cabbages, shred them very finely, first pulling off the outside leaves; mix with them nearly half a pound of salt; tie it up in a thin cloth, and let it hang for twelve hours; then put it into small jars, and pour over it cold vinegar that has been boiled with a few barberries in it. Boil in a quart of vinegar, three bits of ginger, half an ounce of pepper, and a quarter of an ounce of cloves. When cold, pour it over the red cabbage. Tie the jar closely with bladder.

8

SWEETMEATS.

TO CLARIFY SUGAR.

'Mongst salts essential, *sugar* wins the palm,
For taste, for color, and for various use.
O'er all thy works let cleanliness preside,
Child of frugality; and as the scum
Thick mantles o'er the boiling wave, do thou
The scum that mantles carefully remove.

GRAINGER.

Whereof little
More than a little is by much too much.

SHAKSPEARE.

To every three pounds of loaf sugar, allow the
beaten white of an egg and a pint and a half of
water; break the sugar small, put it into a nicely
cleaned brass pan, pour the water over it; let it
stand some time before it be put upon the fire, then
add the beaten white of the egg; stir it till the
sugar be entirely dissolved; when it boils up, pour
in a quarter of a pint of cold water, let it boil up
a second time, take it off the fire, let it settle for
fifteen minutes, carefully take off all the scum, let
it boil again till sufficiently thick; in order to as-

certain which, drop a little from a spoon into a jar of cold water, and if it become quite hard, it is sufficiently done, and the fruit to be preserved must instantly be put in and boiled.

CURRANT JELLY.

He snuffs far off the anticipated joy,
Jelly and ven'son all his thoughts employ.
COWPER.

Currant, grape, and raspberry jelly are all made precisely in the same manner. When the fruit is full ripe, gather it on a dry day. As soon as it is nicely picked, put it into a jar, and cover it down very close. Set the jar in a saucepan, about three parts filled with cold water; put it on a gentle fire, and let it simmer for about half an hour. Take the pan from the fire, and pour the contents of the jar into a jelly-bag, pass the juice through a second time; do not squeeze the bag. To each pint of juice, add a pound and a half of very good lump sugar pounded, when it is put into a preserving pan; set it on the fire, and boil it gently, stirring and skimming it the whole time (about thirty or forty minutes), *i. e.* till no more scum rises, and it is perfectly clear and fine; pour it warm into pots, and when cold, cover them with paper wetted in brandy.

Half a pint of this jelly dissolved in a pint of brandy or vinegar will give you an excellent currant or raspberry brandy or vinegar.

Obs. Jellies from the fruits are made in the same way, and cannot be preserved in perfection without plenty of good sugar. The best way is the cheapest.

APPLE JELLY.

The board was spread with fruits and wine;
With grapes of gold, like those that shine
  On Caslin's hills; pomegranates, full
Of melting sweetness, and the pears
  And sunniest *apples* that Cabul
In all its thousand gardens bears.

                  MOORE.

Pare and mince three dozen juicy, acid apples; put them into a pan; cover them with water, and boil them till very soft; strain them through a thin cloth or flannel bag; allow a pound of loaf sugar to a pint of juice, with the grated peel and juice of six lemons. Boil it for twenty minutes; take off the scum as it rises.

CHERRY JELLY.

With rich conserve of *Visna cherries,*
Of orange flower, and of those berries
That——.

MOORE.

Take the stones and stalks from two pounds of clear, fine, ripe cherries; mix them with a quarter of a pound of red currants, from which the seeds have been extracted; express the juice from these fruits; filter, and mix it with three quarters of a pound of clarified sugar, and one ounce of isinglass. Replace the vessel on the fire with the juice, and add to it a pound and a half of sugar, boiled *à conserve.* Boil together a few times, and then pour the conserve into cases.

CALVES' FEET JELLY.

Nature hates vacuums, as you know,
We, therefore, will descend below,
And fill, with dainties nice and light,
The vacuum in your appetite.
Besides, good wine and dainty fare
Are sometimes known to lighten care;
Nay, man is often brisk or dull,
As the keen stomach's void or full.

To four feet add four quarts of water; let them boil on a slow fire till the flesh is parted from the bones, and the quantity reduced to half; strain it carefully, and the next morning remove the feet and sediment. Add the rind of two lemons, the juice of five lemons, one and a half pounds of white sugar, a stick of cinnamon, a little nutmeg, a pint of sherry wine, half a teacupful of brandy; beat the white of ten eggs to a froth, and put them into the pan with their shells; let it boil ten minutes, when throw in a teacupful of cold water. Strain it through a flannel bag, first dipped into boiling water.

PINEAPPLE PRESERVE.

And the *sun's child*, the *mail'd anana*, yields
His *regal apple* to the ravish'd taste.
GRAINGER.

Pare your pineapple; cut it in small pieces, and leave out the core. Mix the pineapple with half a pound of powdered white sugar, and set it away in a covered dish till sufficient juice is drawn out to stew the fruit in.

Stew the pineapple in the sugar and juice till quite soft, then mash it to a marmalade with the back of a spoon, and set it away to cool; pour it in tumblers, cover them with paper, gum-arabicked on.

EGGS.

OMELET.

Though many, I own, are the evils they've brought us,
　Though R**al*y's here on her very last legs;
Yet who can help loving the land that has taught us
　Six hundred and eighty five ways to dress *eggs!*
MOORE.

Take as many eggs as you think proper; break them into a pan, with some salt and chopped parsley; beat them well, and season them according to taste. Have ready some onion, chopped small; put some butter into a fryingpan, and when it is hot, put in your chopped onion, giving them two or three turns; then add your eggs to it, and fry the whole of a nice brown. You must only fry one side; serve the fried side uppermost.

TO POACH EGGS.

But, after all, what would you have me do,
When, out of twenty, I can please not two?
One likes the pheasant's wing, and one the leg;
The vulgar boil, the learned *poach an egg;*
Hard task to hit the palate of such guests,
When Oldfield loves what Dartineuf detests.
POPE.

The cook who wishes to display her skill in

poaching, must endeavor to procure eggs that have been laid a couple of days; those that are new laid are so milky, that, take all the care you can, your cooking of them will seldom procure you the praise of being a prime poacher. You must have fresh eggs, or it is equally impossible. The beauty of a poached egg is for the yolk to be seen blushing through the white, which should only be just sufficiently hardened to form a transparent veil for the egg. Have some boiling water in a teakettle; pass as much of it through a clean cloth as will half fill a stewpan; break the egg into a cup, and when the water boils remove the stewpan from the stove, and gently slip the egg into it; it must stand till the white is set; then put it on a very moderate fire, and as soon as the water boils, the egg is ready. Take it up with a slicer, and neatly place it on a piece of toast.

BOILED EGGS.

On holydays, an *egg or two* at most;
But her ambition never reached to roast.
CHAUCER.

The fresher laid the better. Put them into boiling water; if you like the white just set, about two minutes' boiling is enough. A new-laid egg will take a little more. If you wish the yolk to be set, it will take three, and to boil it hard for a salad, ten minutes. A new-laid egg will require longer boiling than a stale one by half a minute.

FRIED EGGS.

> Go work, hunt, exercise (he thus begun),
> Then scorn a homely dinner if you can;
> *Fried eggs*, and herbs, and olives, still we see:
> This much is left of old simplicity.
> POPE.

Eggs boiled hard, cut into slices, and fried, may be served as a second course dish, to eat with roast chicken.

EGGS AND BREAD.

> Never go to France,
>   Unless you know the lingo;
> If you do, like me,
>   You'll repent, by jingo.
> Starving like a fool,
>   And silent as a mummy,
> There I stood alone,
>   A nation with a dummy.
>
> Signs I had to make
>   For every little notion;
> Limbs all going like
>   A telegraph in motion;
> If I wanted *bread*,
>   My jaws I set a-going,
> And asked for *new laid eggs*
>   By clapping hands and crowing.

Put half a handful of breadcrumbs into a saucepan, with a small quantity of cream, sugar, and nutmeg, and let it stand till the bread has imbibed all the cream; then break ten eggs into it, and having beaten them up together, fry it like an omelet.

OMELETTE SOUFFLÉ.

"Where is my favorite dish?" he cried;
"Let some one place it by my side!"

DONNE.

Beat up the yolks of eight eggs, and the whites of four (set aside the remaining whites), with a spoonful of water, some salt, sugar, and the juice of a lemon; fry this, and then put it on a dish. Whip the four whites which were set aside to a froth with sugar, and place it over the fried eggs; bake it for a few minutes.

DESSERTS.

PUFF PASTE.

The *puffs* made me light,
And now that's all over, I'm pretty well, thank you.
MOORE.

Weigh an equal quantity of flour and butter, rub rather more than half the flour into one-third of the butter ; add as much cold water as will make it into a stiff paste ; work it until the butter be completely mixed with the flour, make it round, beat it with the rolling-pin, dust it, as also the rolling-pin with flour, and roll it out towards the opposite side of the slab, or paste-board, making it of an equal thickness, then with the point of a knife, put little bits of butter all over it, dust flour over it and under it, fold in all the sides, and roll it up, dust it again with flour, beat it a little, and roll out, always rubbing the rolling-pin with flour, and throwing some underneath the paste to prevent its sticking to the board.

It should be touched as little as possible with the hands.

PYRAMID PASTE.

You that from pliant *paste* would fabrics raise,
Expecting thence to gain immortal praise,
Your knuckles try, and let your sinews know
Their power to knead, and give the form to dough ;
From thence of course the figure will arise,
And elegance adorn the surface of your pies.

KING.

Make a rich puff paste, roll it out a quarter of an inch thick, cut it into five or seven pieces with scalloped tin cutters, which go one within another ; leave the bottom and top piece entire, and cut a bit out of the centre of the others. Place them upon buttered baking tins, and bake them of a light brown. Build them into a pyramid, laying a different preserved fruit upon each piece of paste, and on the top a whole apricot with a sprig of myrtle stuck in it.

FRUIT PIES.

Unless some *sweetness* at the bottom lie,
Who cares for all the crinkling of the pie!

KING.

Fruit pies for family use are generally made with common paste. Allow three quarters of a pound of butter to a pound and a half of flour. Peaches and plums for pies should be cut in half, and the stones taken out. Cherries also should be stoned, and red cherries only should be used for pies. Apples should be cut into very thin slices, and are much improved by a little lemon-peel. Apples stewed previous to baking, should not be done till they break, but only till they are tender. They should then be drained in a cullender, and chopped fine with a knife or edge of a spoon. In making pies of juicy fruit, it is a good way to set a small tea-cup on the bottom crust, and lay the fruit round it. The juice will collect under the cup, and not run out at the edges or top of the pie. The fruit should be mixed with a sufficient quantity of sugar, and piled up in the middle, so as to make the pie highest in the centre.

The upper crust should be pricked with a fork. The edges should be nicely crimped with a knife. If stewed fruit is put in warm, it will make the paste heavy. If your pies are made in the form of shells, the fruit should always be stewed first, or it will not be sufficiently done, as the shells (which should be made of puff paste) must not bake so long as covered pies.

Fruit pies with lids should have loaf sugar grated over them.

MINCE PIES.

When Terence spoke, oraculous and sly,
He'd neither grant the question nor deny,
Pleading for tarts, his thoughts were on *mince pie*.

My poor endeavors view with gracious eye,
To make these lines above a *Christmas pie*.

Two pounds of boiled beef's heart or fresh tongue, or lean fresh beef chopped, when cold; two pounds of beef suet chopped fine, four pounds of pippin apples chopped, two pounds of raisins stoned and chopped, two pounds of currants picked, washed, and dried, two pounds of powdered sugar, one quart of white wine, one quart of brandy, one wine-glass of rose-water, two grated nutmegs, half an ounce of cinnamon, powdered, a quarter of an ounce of mace, powdered, a teaspoonful of salt, two large oranges, and half a pound of citron cut in slips. Pack it closely into stone jars, and tie them over with paper. When it is to be used, add a little more wine.

PLUM PUDDING.

All you who to feasting and mirth are inclined,
Come, here is good news for to pleasure your mind.
Old Christmas is come, for to keep open house:
He scorns to be guilty of starving a mouse.
Then come, boys, and welcome, for diet the chief,—
Plum pudding, goose, capon, minced pies, and roast beef.
The cooks shall be busied, by day and by night,
In roasting and *boiling,* for taste and delight.
Provision is making for beer, ale, and wine,
For all that are willing or ready to dine.
Meantime goes the caterer to fetch in *the chief,*—
Plum pudding, goose, capon, minced pies, and roast beef.

ANCIENT CHRISTMAS CAROL.

One quarter of a pound of beef suet; take out
the strings and skin; chop it to appear like butter;
stone one pound of raisins, one pound of currants,
well washed, dried, and floured, one pound loaf
sugar, rolled and sifted, one pound of flour, eight
eggs well beaten; beat all well together for some
time, then add by degrees two glasses of brandy,
one wine, one rose-water, citron, nutmeg, and cinnamon; beat it all extremely well together, tie it
in a floured cloth very tight, let it boil four hours
constantly; let your sauce be a quarter pound of
butter, beat to a cream, a quarter pound loaf
sugar pounded and sifted; beat in the butter with
a little wine and sugar and nutmeg.

COCOANUT PUDDING.

Whatever was the *best pie* going,
In *that* Ned—trust him—had his finger.

MOORE.

Take the thin brown skin off of a quarter pound
of cocoa, wash it in cold water, and wipe it dry;
grate it fine, stir three and half ounces of butter
and a quarter pound of powdered sugar, to a cream;
add half teaspoonful of rose-water, half glass of wine
and of brandy mixed, to them. Beat the white of six
eggs till they stand alone, and then stir them into
the butter and sugar; afterwards sprinkle in the
grated nut, and stir hard all the time. Put puff
paste into the bottom of the dish, pour in the mixture, and bake it in a moderate oven, half an hour.
Grate loaf sugar over it when cold.

APPLE PUDDING.

Where London's column, pointing to the skies,
Like a tall bully, lifts the head and lies,
There dwelt a citizen of sober fame,
A plain, good man, and Balaam was his name;
Religious, punctual, frugal, and so forth,
His word would pass for more than he was worth;
One solid dish his week-day meal affords,
And *apple pudding* solemnized the Lord's.

POPE.

Make a batter of two eggs, a pint of milk and

three or four spoonfuls of flour; pour it into a deep
dish, and having pared six or eight apples, place
them whole in the batter, and bake them.

HASTY PUDDING.

But man, more fickle, the bold license claims,
In different realms, to give thee different names.
Thee, the soft nations round the warm Levant
Polanta call; the French, of course, Polante.
E'en in thy native regions, how I blush
To hear the Pennsylvanians call thee *mush!*
All spurious appellations, void of truth;
I've better known thee from my earliest youth:
Thy name is *Hasty Pudding!* Thus our sires
Were wont to greet thee from the fuming fires;
And while they argued in thy just defence,
With logic clear, they thus explained the sense:
" In *haste* the boiling caldron, o'er the blaze,
Receives and cooks the ready-powdered maize;
In haste 'tis served, and then in equal *haste*,
With cooling milk, we make the sweet repast.
No carving to be done, no knife to grate
The tender ear, and wound the stony plate;
But the smooth spoon, just fitted to the lip,
And taught with art the yielding mass to dip,
By frequent journeys to the bowl well stored,
Performs the *hasty* honors of the board."

Such is thy name, significant and clear,—
A name, a sound, to every Yankee dear;
But most to me, whose heart and palate chaste
Preserve my pure, hereditary taste.

BARLOW.

YORKSHIRE PUDDING.

The strong table groans
Beneath the smoking sirloin, stretch'd immense
From side to side; in which with desperate knife
They deep incisions make, and talk the while
Of England's glory, ne'er to be defaced
While hence they borrow vigor; or amain
Into the *pudding* plunged at intervals,
If stomach keen can intervals allow,
Relating all the glories of the chase.

THOMSON.

This pudding is especially an excellent accompaniment to a sirloin of beef. Six tablespoonfuls of flour, three eggs, a teaspoonful of salt, and a pint of milk, make a middling stiff batter; beat it up well; take care it is not lumpy. Put a dish under the meat; let the drippings drop into it, till it is quite hot and well greased; then pour in the batter. When the upper surface is browned and set, türn it, that both sides may be brown alike. A pudding an inch thick will take two hours. Serve it under the roast beef, that the juice of the beef may enter it. It is very fine.

SUET PUDDING.

Sir Balaam now, he lives like other folks;
He takes his chirping, and cracks his jokes.
Live like yourself, was soon my lady's word;
And lo! *suet pudding* was seen upon the board.

PObE.

Suet, a quarter of a pound; flour, three tablespoonfuls; eggs two, and a little grated ginger;
milk, half a pint. Mince the suet as fine as possible; roll it with the rolling-pin, so as to mix it
well with the flour; beat up the eggs, mix them
with the milk, and then mix them all together;
wet your cloth well in boiling water, and boil it an
hour and a quarter. Mrs. Glasse has it: " When
you have made your water boil, then put your pudding into your pot."

OATMEAL PUDDING.

Of oats decorticated take two pounds,
And of new milk enough the same to drown;
Of raisins of the sun, stoned, ounces eight;
Of currants, cleanly picked, an equal weight;
Of suet, finely sliced, an ounce at least;
And six eggs, newly taken from the nest:
Season this mixture well with salt and spice;
'Twill make a pudding far exceeding rice;
And you may safely feed on it like farmers,
For the recipe is learned Dr. Harmer's.

EVE'S PUDDING.

If you want a good pudding, mind what you are
 taught :
Take eggs, six in number, when bought for a groat ;
The fruit with which Eve her husband did cozen,
Well pared and well chopped, take at least half a
 dozen ;
Six ounces of bread—let the cook eat the crust—
And crumble the soft as fine as the dust ;
Six ounces of currants from the stalks you must sort,
Lest they husk out your teeth, and spoil all the sport ;
Six ounces of sugar won't make it too sweet,
And some salt and some nutmeg will make it com-
 plete.
Three hours let it boil, without any flutter,
And Adam won't like it without sugar and butter.

ANONYMOUS.

CHARLOTTE DES POMMES.

Charlotte, from rennet apples first did frame
A pie, which still retains her name.
Though common grown, yet with white sugar stewed,
And butter'd right, its goodness is allowed.

KING.

Pare, core, and mince fifteen French rennet
apples ; put them into a frying-pan with some

powdered loaf sugar, a little pounded cinnamon, grated lemon-peel, and two ounces and a half of fresh butter; fry them a quarter of an hour over a quick fire, stirring them constantly. Butter the shape the size the Charlotte is intended to be; cut strips of bread long enough to reach from the bottom to the rim of the shape, so that the whole be lined with bread; dip each bit into melted butter, and put a layer of fried apples, and one of apricot jam or marmalade, and then one of bread dipped into butter; begin and finish with it. Bake it in an oven for an hour. Turn it out to serve.

BATTER PUDDING.

A frugal man, upon the whole,
Yet loved his friend, and had a soul;
Knew what was handsome, and would do't
On just occasion, coûte qui coûte.
He brought him bacon (nothing lean);
Pudding, that might have pleased a dean;
Cheese, such as men of Suffolk make,
But wished it Stilton for his sake.
POPE.

Take six ounces of flour, a little salt, and three eggs; beat it well with a little milk, added by degrees, till the batter becomes smooth; make it the thickness of cream; put it into a buttered and floured bag ; tie it tightly ; boil one and a half hour, or two hours.   Serve with wine sauce.

APPLE DUMPLINGS.

By the rivulet, on the rushes,
Beneath a canopy of bushes,
Colin Blount and Yorkshire Tray
Taste the *dumplings* and the whey.
SMART.

Pare and scoop out the core of six large baking apples; put part of a clove and a little grated lemon-peel inside of each, and enclose them in pieces of puff paste; boil them in nets for the purpose, or bits of linen, for an hour.   Before serving, cut off a small bit from the top of each, and put a teaspoonful of sugar and a bit of fresh butter; replace the bit of paste, and strew over them pounded loaf sugar.

SWEETMEAT FRITTERS.

If chronicles may be believed,
So loved the pamper'd gallant lived,
That with the nuns he always dined
On rarities of every kind ;
Then hoards, occasionally varied,
Of biscuits, *sweetmeats*, nuts, and fruits.

Cut small any sort of candied fruit, and heat it

with a bit of fresh butter, some good milk, and a little grated lemon-peel; when quite hot, stir in enough of flour to make it into a stiff paste; take it off the fire, and work in eight or ten eggs, two at a time. When cold, form the fritters, fry, and serve them with pounded loaf sugar strewed over them.

FRITTERS.

Methinks I scent some *rich repast:*
The savor strengthens with the blast.

GAY.

Take a dozen apricots, òr any other fruit preserved in brandy; drain them in half; then wrap them in wafers, cut round, and previously moistened. Make the batter by putting a glass and a half of water, a grain of salt, and two ounces of fresh butter, into a saucepan. When it boils, stir in sufficient quantity of flour to make it rather a firm batter; keep it stirring three minutes; then pour it into another vessel; dip the fruit in this batter, and fry them; sprinkle them with sugar, then serve.

CREAMS.

ICE CREAM.

After dreaming some hours of the land of Cocaigne,
That Elysium of all that is friand and nice,
Where for hail they have bonbons, and claret for rain,
And the skaters in winter show off on *cream ice.*
MOORE.

Here *ice, like crystal firm,* and never lost,
Tempers hot July with December's frost.
WALLER.

Put a quart of rich cream into a broad pan;
then stir in half a pound of powdered loaf sugar
by degrees, and when all is well mixed, strain it
through a sieve. Put it into a tin that has a close
cover, and set it in a tub. Fill the tub with ice
broken into small pieces, and strew among the ice a
large quantity of salt, taking care that none of the
salt gets into the cream. Scrape the cream down
with a spoon as it freezes round the edges of the
tin. While the cream is freezing, stir in gradually
the juice of two large lemons or the juice of a pint
of mashed strawberries or raspberries. When it is
all frozen, dip the tin in lukewarm water; take
out the cream, and fill your glasses, but not till a
few minutes before you want to use it, as it will
melt very soon.

If you wish to have it in moulds, put the cream into them as soon as it is frozen in the tin.

Set the moulds in a tub of ice and salt. Just before you want to use the cream, take the moulds out of the tub, wipe or wash the salt carefully from the outside, dip the moulds into lukewarm water, and turn out the cream. You may flavor a quart of ice cream with two ounces of sweet almonds, and one ounce of bitter almonds, blanched, and beaten in a mortar with a little rose-water to a smooth paste.

Stir in the almond gradually, while the cream is freezing.

WHIPPED CREAM.

Pudding our parson eats, the squire loves hare,
But *whipped cream* is my Buxoma's fare,
While she loves *whipped cream*, capon ne'er shall be,
Nor hare, nor beef, nor pudding, food for me.
GAY.

Sweeten with pounded loaf sugar a quart of cream, and to it a lump of sugar which has been rubbed upon the peel of two fine lemons or little oranges ; or flavor it with orange flower water, a little essence of roses, the juice of strawberries, or any other fruit. Whisk the cream well in a large pan, and as the froth rises, take it off, and lay it on a sieve placed over another pan, and return the cream which drains from the froth till all is whisked; then heap it upon a dish, or put it into glasses.

BOILED CUSTARDS.

And *boiled custard*, take its merit in brief,
Makes a noble dessert, where the dinner's roast beef.

Boil a pint of milk with lemon-peel and cinnamon; mix a pint of cream, and the yolks of five eggs well beaten; when the milk tastes of the seasoning, sweeten enough for the whole; pour it into the cream, stirring it well; then give the custard a simmer till of a proper thickness. Do not let it boil; stir the whole time one way; then season with a large spoonful of peach-water, and two teaspoonfuls of brandy or a little ratafia. If you wish your custards extremely rich, put no milk, but a quart of cream.

ORANGE CUSTARDS.

With *orange custards* and the juicy pine,
On choicest melons and sweet grapes they dine.
JONSON.

Sweeten the strained juice of ten oranges with pounded loaf sugar, stir it over the fire till hot, take off the scum, and when nearly cold, add to it the beaten yolks of twelve eggs and a pint of cream;

put it into a saucepan, and stir it over a slow fire till it thickens.   Serve it in cups.

CUSTARDS OR CREAMS.

But nicer cates, her dainty's boasted fare,
The *jellied cream* or custards, daintiest food,
Or cheesecake, or the cooling syllabub,
For Thyrses she prepares.
DODSLEY.

Whisk for one hour the whites of two eggs, together with two tablespoonfuls of raspberry or red currant syrup or jelly ; lay it in any form of a custard or cream, piled up to imitate rock.   It may be served in a cream round it.

ALMOND CREAMS.

And from *sweet kernels* pressed,
She tempers *dulcet creams*.
MILTON.

Blanch and pound to a paste, with rose-water, six ounces of almonds ; mix them with a pint and a half of cream which has been boiled with the peel of a small lemon ; add two well-beaten eggs, and stir the whole over the fire till it be thick, taking care not to allow it to boil ; sweeten it, and when nearly cold, stir in a tablespoonful of orange-flower or rose-water.

MISCELLANEOUS.

YEAST.

Not with the leaven, as of old,
Of sin and malice fed,
But with unfeigned sincerity.

One dozen of potatoes, two cupfuls of hops; put them together in a bag, and place them in a pot with two quarts of water; let it boil till the potatoes are done; a cupful of salt, a ladle of flour; then pour the boiling water over it, then let it stand till lukewarm; add a cupful of old yeast, cover it up, and put near the fire till it foments.

BREAD.

His diet was of *wheaten bread.*
COWPER.

Mixt with the rustic throng, see ruddy maids,
Some taught with dextrous hand to twirl the wheel,
Some expert
To raise from *leavened wheat the kneaded loaf.*
DODSLEY.

Her *bread* is deemed such dainty fare,
That ev'ry prudent traveller
His wallet loads with many a crust.
                              COWPER.

Like the *loaf* in the Tub's pleasant tale,
That was fish, flesh, and custard, good claret and ale,
It comprised every flavor, was all and was each,
Was grape and was pineapple, nectarine and peach.
                              LOVILOND.

Mix with six pounds of sifted flour one ounce of salt, nearly half a pint of fresh sweet yeast as it comes from the brewery, and a sufficient quantity of warmed milk to make the whole into a stiff dough, work and knead it well on a board, on which a little flour has been strewed, for fifteen or twenty minutes, then put it into a deep pan, cover it with a warmed towel, set it before the fire, and let it rise for an hour and a half or perhaps two hours; cut off a piece of this sponge or dough; knead it well for eight or ten minutes, together with flour sufficient to keep it from adhering to the board, put it into small tins, filling them three quarters full; dent the rolls all around with a knife, and let them stand a few minutes before putting them in the oven.

The remainder of the dough must then be worked up for loaves, and baked either in or out of shape.

10*

RYE AND INDIAN BREAD.

Of wine she never tasted through the year,
But white and black was all her homely cheer,
Brown bread and milk (but first she skimmed her bowls),
And rasher of singed bacon on the coals.

CHAUCER.

Sift two quarts of rye, and two quarts of Indian meal, and mix them well together. Boil three pints of milk; pour it boiling upon the meal; add two teaspoonfuls of salt, and stir the whole very hard. Let it stand till it becomes of only a lukewarm heat, and then stir in half a pint of good, fresh yeast; if from the brewery and quite fresh, a smaller quantity will suffice. Knead the mixture into a stiff dough, and set it to rise in a pan. Cover it with a thick cloth that has been previously warmed, and set it near the fire. When it is quite light, and has cracked all over the top, make it into two loaves; put them into a moderate oven, and bake them two hours and a half.

BUTTER.

Vessels large
And broad, by the sweet hand of neatness clean'd,
Meanwhile, in decent order ranged appear,
The milky treasure, strain'd thro' filtering lawn,
Intended to receive.   At early day,
Sweet slumber shaken from her opening lids,
My lovely Patty to her dairy hies;
There, from the surface of expanded bowls
She skims the floating cream, and to her churn
Commits the rich consistence; nor disdains,
Though soft her hand, though delicate her frame,
To urge the rural toil, fond to obtain
The country housewife's humble name and praise.
Continued agitation separates soon
The unctuous particles; with gentler strokes
And artful, soon they coalesce; at length
Cool water pouring from the limpid spring
Into a smooth glazed vessel, deep and wide,
She gathers the loose fragments to a heap,
Which in the cleansing wave, well wrought and
      press'd,
To one consistent golden mass, receives
The sprinkled seasoning, and of pats or pounds
The fair impression, the neat shape assumes.

DODSLEY.

COTTAGE CHEESE.

> Warm from the cow she pours
> The milky flood.   An acid juice infused,
> From the dried stomach drawn of suckling calf,
> Coagulates the whole.   Immediate now
> Her spreading hands bear down the gathering curd,
> Which hard and harder grows, till, clear and thin,
> The green whey rises separate.
>
> DODSLEY.

Warm three half pints of cream with one half pint of milk, and put a little rennet to it; keep it covered in a warm place till it is curdled; have a proper mould with holes, either of china or any other; put the curds into it to drain, about one hour or less.   Serve it with a good plain cream, and pounded sugar over it.

CAKES.

BUCKWHEAT CAKES.

Do, dear James, mix up the cakes:
Just one quart of meal it takes;
Pour the water on the pot,
Be careful it is not too hot;
Sift the meal well through your hand,
Thicken well—don't let it stand;
Stir it quick,—clash, clatter, clatter!
O what light, delicious batter!
Now listen to the next command:
On the dresser let it stand
Just three quarters of an hour,
To feel the gently rising power
Of powders, melted into yeast,
To lighten well this precious feast.
See, now it rises to the brim!
Quick, take the ladle, dip it in;
So let it rest, until the fire
The griddle heats as you desire.
Be careful that the coals are glowing,
No smoke around its white curls throwing;
Apply the suet, softly, lightly;
The griddle's black face shines more
    brightly.

Now pour the batter on; delicious!
Don't, dear James, think me officious,
But lift the tender edges lightly;
Now turn it over quickly, sprightly.
'Tis done! Now on the white plate lay it:
Smoking hot, with butter spread,
'Tis quite enough to turn our head!

JOHNNY CAKES.

Some talk of hoecake, fair Virginia's pride!
Rich *Johnny cake* this mouth has often tried;
Both please me well, their virtues much the same;
Alike their fabric, as allied their fame.

BARLOW.

A quart of sifted Indian meal, and a handful of
wheat flour sifted; mix them; three eggs, well
beaten; two tablespoonfuls of fresh brewer's yeast,
or flour of home made yeast, a teaspoonful of salt,
and a quart of milk.

MUFFINS.

Friend, I am a shrewd observer, and will guess
What cakes you doat on for your favorite mess.

ARMSTRONG.

Take a pint of warm milk, and a quarter pint of
thick small-beer yeast; strain them into a pan, and

add sufficient flour to make it like a batter; cover
it over, and let it stand in a warm place until it
has risen; then add a quarter of a pint of warm
milk, and an ounce of butter rubbed in some flour
quite fine; mix them well together; add sufficient
flour to make it into a dough; cover it over.   Let
it stand half an hour; work it up again; break it
into small pieces, roll them up quite round, and
cover them over for a quarter of an hour, then
bake them.

PANCAKES.

With all her haughty looks, the time I've seen
When the proud damsel has more humble been;
When with nice airs she hoist the *pancake* round,
And dropt it, hapless fair! upon the ground.
                                    SHENSTONE.

To three tablespoonfuls of flour add six well-
beaten eggs, three tablespoonfuls of white wine,
four ounces of melted butter nearly cold, the same
quantity of pounded loaf sugar, half a grated nutmeg, and a pint of cream.   Mix it well, beating the
batter for some time, and pour it thin over the pan.

PLUM-CAKE.

> First in place,
> *Plum-cake* is seen o'er smaller pastry ware,
> And ice on that.
>
> SWIFT.

Pick two pounds of currants very clean, and wash them, draining them through a cullender. Wipe them in a towel, spread them out in a large dish, and set them near the fire or in the hot sun to dry, placing the dish in a slanting position. Having stoned two pounds of best raisins, cut them in half, and when all are done, sprinkle them well with sifted flour, to prevent their sinking to the bottom of the cake. When the currants are dry, sprinkle them also with flour.

Pound the spice, two tablespoonfuls of cinnamon, two nutmegs, powdered; sift and mix the cinnamon and nutmeg together. Mix also a large glass of wine and brandy, half a glass of rose-water in a tumbler or cup. Cut a pound of citron in slips; sift a pound of flour in a broad dish, sift a pound of powdered white sugar into a deep earthen pan, and cut a pound of butter into it. Warm it near the fire, if the weather is too cold for it to mix easily. Stir the butter and sugar to a cream; beat twelve eggs as light as possible; stir them into the butter and sugar alternately with the flour; stir very hard; add gradually the spice and liquor. Stir the raisins and currants alternately in the mixture, taking care that they are well floured. Stir the whole as hard as possible, for ten minutes after the ingredients are in.

Cover the bottom and sides of a large tin or earthen pan with sheets of white paper well buttered, and put into it some of the mixture. Then spread some citron on it, which must not be cut too small; next put a layer of the mixture, and then a layer of citron, and so on till all is in, having a layer of mixture at the top.

This cake will require four or five hours baking, in proportion to its thickness.

Ice it next day.

LAFAYETTE GINGERBREAD.

Must see Rheims, much famed, 'tis said,
For making kings and *gingerbread*.
MOORE.

Five eggs, half pound of brown sugar, half pound fresh butter, a pint of sugarhouse molasses, a pound and a half of flour, four tablespoonfuls of ginger, two large sticks of cinnamon, three dozen grains of allspice, three dozen of cloves, juice and grated peel of two lemons. Stir the butter and sugar to a cream; beat the eggs very well; pour the molasses at once into the butter and sugar. Add the ginger and other spice, and stir all well together. Put in the eggs and flour alternately, stirring all the time. Stir the whole very hard, and put in the lemon at the last. When the whole is mixed, stir it till very light. Butter an earthen pan, or a thick tin or iron one, and put the gingerbread in it. Bake it in a moderate oven an hour or more, according to its thickness, or you may bake it in small cakes or little tins.

SHREWSBURY CAKES.

And here each season do *those cakes* abide,
Whose honored names the inventive city own,
Rendering through Britain's isle Salopia's praises known.
SHENSTONE.

Sift one pound of sugar, some pounded cinnamon and a nutmeg grated, into three pounds of flour, the finest sort; add a little rose-water to three eggs well beaten; mix these with the flour, &c.; then pour into it as much butter melted as will make it a good thickness to roll out.

Stir it well, and roll thin; cut it into such shapes as you like. Bake on tins.

HONEY-CAKE.

In vain the circled loaves attempt to lie
Concealed in flaskets from my curious eye;
In vain the cheeses, offspring of the pail,
Or *honeyed cakes*, which gods themselves regale.
PARNELL.

One pound and a half of dried sifted flour, three quarters of a pound of honey, half a pound of finely powdered loaf sugar, a quarter of a pound of citron, and half an ounce of orange-peel cut small, of powdered ginger and cinnamon, three quarters of an ounce. Melt the sugar with the honey, and mix in the other ingredients; roll out the paste, and cut it into small cakes of any form.

NAPLES BISCUITS.

Though I've consulted Holinshed and Stow,
I find it very difficult to know
Who, to refresh the attendants to a grave,
Burnt claret first or *Naples biscuit* gave.
KING.

Put three quarters of a pound of fine flour to a pound of powdered sugar; sift both together three times; then add six eggs beaten well, and a spoonful of rose-water; when the oven is nearly hot, bake them.

GINGERBREAD.

Whence oft with sugared cates she doth 'em greet,
And *gingerbread*, if rare, now certes doubly sweet.
                                        SHENSTONE.

To three quarters of a pound of treacle, beat one
egg strained; mix four ounces of brown sugar, half
an ounce of ginger sifted, of cloves, mace, allspice,
and nutmeg, a quarter of an ounce; beat all as
fine as possible; melt one pound of butter, and mix
with the above; add as much flour as will knead it
into a pretty stiff paste; roll it out, and cut it in
cakes.

SPONGE CAKE.

On *cake* luxuriously I dine,
And drink the fragrance of the vine,
Studious of elegance and ease,
Myself alone I seek to please.
                                        GAY.

Take the juice and grated rind of a lemon, twelve
eggs, twelve ounces of finely pounded loaf sugar,
the same of dried and sifted flour; then, beat
the yolks of ten eggs; add the sugar by degrees, and beat it till it will stand when dropped
from the spoon; put in at separate times the
two other eggs, yolks, and whites; whisk the ten

whites for eight minutes, and mix in the lemon-juice, and when quite stiff, take as much as the whisk will lift, and put it upon the yolks and sugar, which must be beaten all the time; mix in lightly all the flour and grated peel, and pour it gradually over the whites; stir it together, and bake it in a large buttered tin or small ones; do not more than half fill them.

SUGAR BISCUITS.

This happy hour elapsed and gone,
The time of drinking tea comes on.
The kettle filled, the water boiled,
The cream provided, the *biscuits* piled,
And lamp prepared; I straight engage
The Lilliputian equipage
Of dishes, sauces, spoons, and tongs,
And all the et ceteras which-thereto belongs.
                                        DODSLEY.

The weight of eight eggs in finely pounded loaf sugar, and of four in dried flour; beat separately the whites and yolks; with the yolks beat the sugar for half an hour; then add the whites and the flour, and a little grated nutmeg, lemon-peel, or pounded cinnamon. Bake them as French biscuits.

DERBY CAKE.

Some bring a capon, some *Derby cake*,
Some nuts, some apples, some that think they make
The better cheesecakes, bring them.

Rub in with the hand one pound of butter into
two pounds of sifted flour; put one pound of currants, one pound of good moist sugar, and one egg;
mix all together with half pint of milk; roll it out
thin, and cut it into round cakes with a cutter;
lay them on a clean baking plate, and put them
into a middling heated oven for about ten minutes.

CRACKNELS.

However, you shall home with me to night,
Forget your cares, and revel in delight;
I have in store a pint or two of wine,
Some *cracknels*, and the remnant of a chine.
                                    SWIFT.

Blanch half a pound of sweet almonds, and pound
them to a fine paste, adding to them by degrees six
eggs, when thoroughly pounded; pour on them a
pound of powdered sugar, the same of butter, and
the rinds of two lemons grated; beat up these ingredients in the mortar; put a pound of flour on a slab,
and having poured the almond paste upon it, knead

them together till they are well incorporated; roll it out, and cut the cracknels into such forms as you think proper; rub them with yolk of egg, and strew over them powdered sugar or cinnamon; then lay them on a buttered tin, and bake them in a moderate oven, taking great care they do not burn.

CHEESECAKES.

Treat here, ye shepherds blithe! your damsels sweet,
For pies and *cheesecakes* are for damsels meet.

GAY.

Put two quarts of new milk into a stewpan; set it near the fire, and stir in two tablespoonfuls of rennet; let it stand till it is set (this will take about an hour); break it well with your hand, and let it remain half an hour longer; then pour off the whey, and put the curd into a cullender to drain; when quite dry, put it in a mortar, and pound it quite smooth; then add four ounces of powdered sugar, and three ounces of fresh butter; oil it first by putting it in a little potting pot, and setting it near the fire; stir it all well together; beat the yolks of four eggs in a basin with a little nutmeg grated, lemon-peel, and a glass of brandy; add this to the curd, with two ounces of currants washed and picked; stir it all well together; have your tins ready lined with puff paste, about a quarter of an inch thick ; notch them all round the edge, and fill each with the curd.

Bake them twenty minutes.

BRIDE CAKE.

The bridal came; great the feast,
And good the *bride cake* and the priest.
SMART.

Take four pounds of fresh butter, two pounds of loaf sugar, pounded and sifted fine, a quarter of an ounce of mace and the same quantity of nutmegs ; to every pound of flour put eight eggs ; wash and pick four pounds of currants, and dry them before the fire ; blanch a pound of sweet almonds, and cut them lengthways very thin, a pound of citron, a pound of candied orange, a pound of candied lemon, and half pint of brandy ; first work the butter to a cream ; then beat in your sugar a quarter of an hour ; beat the white of your eggs to a very strong froth ; mix them with your sugar and butter ; beat the yolks half an hour at least, and mix them with your cake ; then put in your flour, mace, and nutmeg ; keep beating it till your oven is ready ; put in your brandy ; beat the currants and almonds lightly in ; tie three sheets of paper round the bottoms of your hoops, to keep it from running out; rub it well with butter; put in your cake and the sweetmeats in three layers, with cake between every layer; after it is risen and colored, cover it with paper.

It takes three hours baking.

KISSES.

"I never give a *kiss*," says Prue,
  "To naughty man, for I abhor it."
She will not give a *kiss*, 'tis true,
  She'll take one, though, and thank you for it.
                    FROM THE FRENCH.

One pound of the best loaf sugar, powdered and sifted, the whites of four eggs, twelve drops of essence of lemon, a teacup of currant jelly. Beat the whites of four eggs till they stand alone. Then beat in gradually the sugar, a teaspoonful at a time. Add the essence of lemon, and beat the whole very hard. Lay a wet sheet of paper on the bottom of a square tin pan. Drop on it at equal distances a small teaspoonful of currant jelly. With a large spoon, pile some of the beaten white of eggs and sugar on each lump of jelly, so as to cover it entirely. Drop on the mixture as evenly as possible, so as to make the kisses of a round

smooth shape.   Set them in a cool oven, and as
soon as they are colored, they are done.   Then
take them out, and place two bottoms together.
Lay them lightly on a sieve, and dry them in a
cool oven, till the two bottoms stick fast together,
so as to form one oval or ball.

SWEET MACAROONS.

Where *cakes* luxuriant pile the spacious dish,
  And purple nectar glads the festive hour,
The guest, without a want, without a wish,
  Can yield no room to music's soothing power.
                                    JOHNSON.

Blanch a pound of sweet almonds ; throw them
into cold water for a few minutes ; lay them in a
napkin to dry, and leave them for twenty-four
hours ; at the end of that time, pound them, a handful at a time, adding occasionally some white of
egg, till the whole is reduced to a fine paste ; then
take two pounds of the best lump sugar ; pound
and sift it ; then put it to the almonds with the
grated rinds of two lemons ; beat these ingredients
together in the mortar, adding, one at a time, as
many eggs as you find necessary to moisten the
paste, which should be thin, but not too much so,
as in that case it would run ; your paste being
ready, take out a little in a spoon, and lay the

macaroons on sheets of white paper, either round or oval, as you please; lay them at least an inch apart, because they spread in baking, and, if put nearer, would touch.

The whole of your paste being used, place the sheets of paper on tins in a moderate oven for three quarters of an hour.

This kind of cake requires great care.

SYLLABUB.

Mountown! the Muses' most delicious theme,
O, may thy codlins ever swim in cream!
The rasp and strawberries in Bordeaux drown,
To add a redder tincture to their own!
Thy white wine, sugar, milk, together club,
To make that gentle viand—*syllabub!*

KING.

Not all thy plate, how formed soe'er it be,
Can please my palate like a bowl of thee.

BARLOW.

In a large china bowl put a pint of port and a pint of sherry, or other white wine; sugar to taste. Milk the bowl full; in twenty minutes cover it pretty high with clouted cream; grate over it nutmeg; put pounded cinnamon and nonpareil comfits. It is very good without the nonpareil comfits.

BEER OR ALE.

O, Peggy, Peggy! when thou goest to brew,
Consider well what you're about to do ;
Be very wise, very sedately think
That what you're now going to make is *drink;*
Consider who must drink that drink, and then
What 'tis to have the praise of *honest* men ;
For surely, Peggy, while that drink does last,
'Tis Peggy will be *toasted or disgraced.*
Then if thy *ale* in glass thou wouldst confine,
To make its sparkling rays in beauty shine,
Let thy clean bottle be entirely dry,
Lest a white substance to the surface fly,
And floating there disturb the curious eye ;
But this great maxim must be understood,
" *Be sure, nay very sure, thy cork be good.*"
Then future ages shall of Peggy tell,
That nymph that *brewed and bottled ale so well!*
KING.

Twelve bushels of malt to the hogshead for beer,
eight for ale; for either, pour the whole quantity
of water, hot, but not boiling, on at once, and let
it infuse three hours, close covered ; mash it in the
first half hour, and let it stand the remainder of
the time. Run it on the hops, previously infused
in water ; for beer, three quarters of a pound to a

bushel; if for ale, half a pound.   Boil them with
the wort, two hours, from the time it begins to boil.
Cool a pailful; then add three quarts of yeast,
which will prepare it for putting to the rest when
ready next day; but, if possible, put together the
same night.   Sun, as usual.   Cover the bunghole
with paper, when the beer has done working; and
when it is to be stopped, have ready a pound and
a half of hops, dried before the fire; put them into
the bunghole, and fasten it up.

Let it stand twelve months in casks, and twelve
in bottles before it be drank.   It will keep, and be
very fine, eight or ten years.   It should be brewed
in the beginning of March.   Great care must be
taken that bottles are perfectly prepared, and *the
corks are of the best sort.*

The ale will be ready in three or four months,
and if the vent-peg be never removed, it will have
spirit and strength to the last.   Allow two gallons
of water, at first, for waste.

After the beer or ale is run from the grains,
pour a hogshead and a half for the twelve bushels;
and a hogshead of water, if eight were brewed.
Mash, and let stand; and then boil, &c.

ORIGIN OF MINT JULEPS.

'Tis said that the gods, on Olympus of old,
  (And who the bright legend profanes with a
    doubt!)
One night, 'mid their revels, by Bacchus were told,
  That his last butt of nectar had somehow run out.

But determined to send round the goblet once more,
  They sued to the fairer mortals for aid
In composing a draught, which till drinking were
    o'er,
  Should cast every wine ever drank in the shade.

Grave Ceres herself blithely yielded her corn,
  And the spirit that lives in each amber-hued
    grain,
And which first had its birth from the dews of the
    morn,
  Was taught to steal out in bright dew-drops again.

Pomona, whose choicest of fruits on the board
  Were scattered profusely, in every one's reach,
When called on a tribute to cull from the hoard,
  Express'd the mild juice of the delicate peach.

The liquids were mingled, while Venus looked on,
   With glances so fraught with sweet magical power,
That the honey of Hybla, e'en when they were gone,
   Has never been missed in the draught from that
     hour.

Flora then from her bosom of fragrancy shook,
   And with roseate fingers pressed down in the bowl,
All dripping and fresh as it came from the brook,
   The *herb* whose aroma should flavor the whole.

The draught was delicious, each god did exclaim,
   Though something yet wanting they all did be-
     wail;
But *juleps* the drink of immortals became,
   When Jove himself added a handful of hail.

                 HOFFMAN.

PUNCH.

Four elements, joined in
   An emulous strife,
Fashion the world, and
   Constitute life.

From the sharp citron
   The starry juice pour;
Acid to life is
   The innermost core.

Now, let the sugar
   The bitter one meet;
Still be life's bitter
   Tamed down with the sweet!

Let the bright water
   Flow into the bowl;
Water, the calm one,
   Embraces the whole.

Drops from the spirit
　　Pour quick'ning within,
Life but its life from
　　The spirit can win.

Haste, while it gloweth,
　　Your vessels to bring;
The wave has but virtue
　　Drunk hot from the spring.

TRANSLATED FROM SCHILLER.

INDEX.